CW00324520

100 Favourite Poems

100 Favourite Poems

Chosen by LAURENCE COTTERELL

PIATKUS

First published in 1989 by
Judy Piatkus (Publishers) Ltd,
5 Windmill Street, London W1P 1HF

Reprinted 1990 (twice)

British Library Cataloguing in Publication Data
100 favourite poems.
1. Poetry in English. Anthologies
I. Cotterell, Laurence
821'.008

ISBN 0-86188-898-7

Designed and illustrated by Paul Saunders
Phototypeset in Compugraphic Palatino by
Action Typesetting Ltd, Gloucester
Printed and bound in Great Britain by
Butler and Tanner Ltd, Frome, Somerset

Contents

List of Paintings

INTRODUCTION

'Choose a hundred favourite poems!' said the publisher amiably. Alas, the problem lies not in finding a hundred but in trying to whittle down from a thousand possibilities, all of them commanding a constant and appreciative audience. It is good that this should be so, and that there should be no closely defined or restricted list of what is 'popular'. My listening and recording during a long life stand me in good stead. This selection consists of a hundred poems I have heard quoted again and again, sometimes in unexpected company and situations, from men and women of the widest variety of social, cultural and occupational backgrounds. It is a personal selection, as all anthologies are bound to be. It is derived from spontaneous utterances heard in schools and shops, in pubs and different public places, in homes and at social gatherings. (For some reason, those who work in transport – bus conductors, taxi drivers, haulage drivers and railway staff among them – seem to have a special memory for favourite poems!)

I am sure that everyone who picks up this book could compile a list of what are his or her own hundred 'favourite' poems, and I'm equally sure that there would be a great deal of common ground. My hope is that many of your favourites find a place in my selection!

Academic and dictionary definitions of 'poetry' are vague and unsatisfying. But if we accept poetry as being the *word* music of human life, then it must surely be men and women who *live* life (so often patronisingly described by the politicians as 'ordinary men and women') who are the ultimate judges. We may not understand all that we like, but it is sufficient that we get a warm feeling – an emotional impulse – from certain poems. The reaction might differ from one person to another when confronted with, say, John Clare's 'First Love' or Housman's 'Fancy's Knell', to mention but two entries in this selection, and that is how it should be.

There is no human experience or situation – physical, mental or spiritual – that has not been described vividly and with incomparable force in poetry. Whether or not God exists, Man has perhaps come as close to Him or His concept in poetry as in any other element. There is no condition or emotion from misery to ecstasy that fails to find a hundred reflections in published verse. In going through the mass of 'possibles' for this selection, I had no conscious intention of balancing categories or giving priority to one emotion over another. The poems were chosen without thought of classification, which was only made later, with headings related to what had been selected. In the event, the most 'populated' categories turned out to be Love and

Reflection, with Nature, War, the Lyrical and Humour (with Satire) following abreast, followed in turn by a reasonable showing for the Spiritual and Journeyings. And in order that the Love section should not over-dominate the rest, some borderline cases which came appropriately in that category were switched to others where they sit with equal propriety. Perhaps, having emerged fortuitously and unforced, these *are* the main and most significant human emotions.

As you'll see, I decided to leave out long ballads for the most part, and poems that tend to get widely parodied. 'Gunga Din' and 'The Charge of the Light Brigade' are good examples. I have also omitted the works of poets – often famous poets – who, while they properly live on in critical memory and appreciation from generation to generation, write in an esoteric fashion and appeal only to a minority at any given time.

However, the views and assessments of the critics and intellectuals must always be respected since it is for them to weigh up the new, the adventurous and the experimental. They are needed to sift and to discount the dross, while seeing that the worthwhile does not disappear – however small the potential audience may appear to be. Yet the true intellectual will not despise a beautiful poem simply because it has become a favourite piece with tens of thousands of people. Notable examples in this selection are the Shakespeare Sonnets and Coleridge's 'Kubla Khan', quotable and quoted so widely while at the same time being included in even the most erudite anthologies.

I have had to give myself various rules in order to make my selection and I have therefore allowed for no more than two poems from any one particular hand. It would be easy to make up a hundred favourite poems from Shakespeare and a dozen others, but a wider net of tastes and interests is visualised here. A reminder of the delights exemplified by Yeats' 'When you are Old', for example, can always send the admirer, flavour-buds aroused, back to the poet's collected works. In fact, I would be extremely happy if it should do so.

When I was Chairman of the Poetry Society, I wrote to one very popular and very funny versifier, thanking her for building a bridge in the direction of poetry – even if her own material would hardly be accepted as such in Hampstead and its spiritual suburbs! I got a nice, goodnatured reply. When you read this collection, you may recognise entries which, for you, have been a bridge to the appreciation of more polished works.

Poetry is the one art form at which the English are supreme. And when I say 'English', I mean all those, whatever their origins or backgrounds, who use the English language as a means of expression. Thus, as I see it, there is

no such thing as, for example, an 'American' poet. If the poet is writing in English, however bizarre or adapted the language may be, then he is an *English* poet of American or other extraction, although his or her work will be enriched and coloured (enriching the body of English poetry in turn) by the special conditions of the country and environment concerned. In this selection there is a sprinkling of poems from English-speaking countries other than the United Kingdom, though naturally enough the long literary history of these crowded islands means that its 'popular' poems have been established as such elsewhere in the world. However, the reverse procedure increases steadily in strength and volume, so that another '100 Favourite Poems' in some years' time may well show a heavier proportion of works from those born in other countries.

Very few living poets are represented simply because they have not, for the most part, had time to become truly 'popular', although I am particularly reluctant to leave out Patricia Beer and a good many other contemporary writers who will doubtless figure in any selection of 'favourite poems' in years to come. It would not be difficult for me, or any other observers of the poetry scene, to compile right here and now, with confidence, a prophetic list of '100 Populist Poems' – those which will assuredly become popular very soon.

With only a layman's eye for art, I was also asked to choose some sixteen paintings that might march with the poetry, conveying with their combined presentation the same kind of general impression. But since these poems take a vast range of human reactions, it has been impossible to do more than choose paintings that are somehow, taken as a whole, evocative of the sentiments and situations exemplified in the poems. With a field of possibles as wide in painting as in poetry itself, this can only be an arbitrary selection but I hope it is one which you will enjoy.

LAURENCE COTTERELL
May 1989

LOVE

My Love in Her Attire

MY LOVE in her attire doth show her wit,
  It doth so well become her:
For every season she hath dressings fit,
  For winter, spring, and summer.
No beauty she doth miss
  When all her robes are on;
But Beauty's self she is
  When all her robes are gone.

ANON

Love Me Not

LOVE me not for comely grace,
For my pleasing eye or face,
Nor for any outward part,
No, nor for my constant heart;
For those may fail or turn to ill,
  So thou and I shall sever.
Keep therefore a true woman's eye,
And love me still, but know not why,
So hast thou the same reason still
  To dote upon me ever.

ANON

A Subaltern's Love-song

MISS J. Hunter Dunn, Miss J. Hunter Dunn,
Furnish'd and burnish'd by Aldershot sun,
What strenuous singles we played after tea,
We in the tournament — you against me!

Love-thirty, love-forty, oh! weakness of joy,
The speed of a swallow, the grace of a boy,
With carefullest carelessness, gaily you won,
I am weak from your loveliness, Joan Hunter Dunn.

Miss Joan Hunter Dunn, Miss Joan Hunter Dunn,
How mad I am, sad I am, glad that you won
The warm-handled racket is back in its press,
But my shock-headed victor, she loves me no less.

Her father's euonymus shines as we walk,
And swing past the summer-house, buried in talk,
And cool the verandah that welcomes us in
To the six-o'clock news and a lime-juice and gin.

The scent of the conifers, sound of the bath,
The view from my bedroom of moss-dappled path,
As I struggle with double-end evening tie,
For we dance at the Golf Club, my victor and I.

On the floor of her bedroom lie blazer and shorts
And the cream-coloured walls are be-trophied with sports,
And westering, questioning settles the sun
On your low-leaded window, Miss Joan Hunter Dunn.

The Hillman is waiting, the light's in the hall,
The pictures of Egypt are bright on the wall,
My sweet, I am standing beside the oak stair
And there on the landing's the light on your hair.

By roads 'not adopted', by woodlanded ways,
She drove to the club in the later summer haze,
Into nine-o'clock Camberley, heavy with bells
And mushroomy, pine-woody, evergreen smells.

Miss Joan Hunter Dunn, Miss Joan Hunter Dunn,
I can hear from the car-park the dance has begun.
Oh! full Surrey twilight! importunate band!
Oh! strongly adorable tennis-girl's hand!

Around us are Rovers and Austins afar,
Above us, the intimate roof of the car,
And here on my right is the girl of my choice,
With the tilt of her nose and the chime of her voice,

And the scent of her wrap, and the words never said,
And the ominous, ominous dancing ahead.
We sat in the car park till twenty to one
And now I'm engaged to Miss Joan Hunter Dunn.

SIR JOHN BETJEMAN (1906–1984)

Remembrance

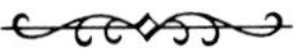

COLD in the earth — and the deep snow piled above thee,
Far, far, removed, cold in the dreary grave!
Have I forgot, my only Love, to love thee,
Severed at last by Time's all-severing wave?

Now, when alone, do my thoughts no longer hover
Over the mountains, on that northern shore,
Resting their wings where heath and fern-leaves cover
That noble heart for ever, ever more?

Cold in the earth, and fifteen wild Decembers
From those brown hills have melted into spring:
Faithful, indeed, is the spirit that remembers
After such years of change and suffering!

Sweet Love of youth, forgive, if I forget thee,
While the world's tide is bearing me along;
Other desires and other hopes beset me,
Hopes which obscure, but cannot do thee wrong!

No later light has lightened up my heaven,
No second morn has ever shone for me;
All my life's bliss from thy dear life was given,
All my life's bliss is in the grave with thee.

But, when the days of golden dreams had perished,
And even Despair was powerless to destroy;
Then did I learn how existence could be cherished,
Strengthened, and fed without the aid of joy.

Then did I check the tears of useless passion —
Weaned my young soul from yearning after thine;
Sternly denied its burning wish to hasten
Down to that tomb already more than mine.

And, even yet, I dare not let it languish,
Dare not indulge in memory's rapturous pain;
Once drinking deep of that divinest anguish,
How could I seek the empty world again?

EMILY BRONTE (1818–1848)

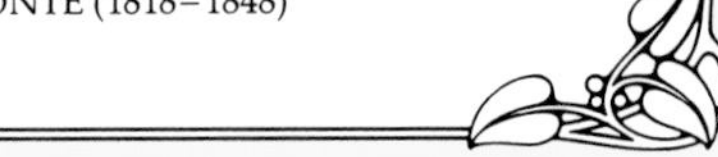

Sonnet XLIII:
How Do I Love Thee?

How do I love thee? Let me count the ways.
I love thee to the depth and breadth and height
My soul can reach, when feeling out of sight
For the ends of Being and ideal Grace.
I love thee to the level of every day's
Most quiet need, by sun and candlelight.
I love thee freely, as men strive for Right;
I love thee purely, as they turn from Praise.
I love thee with the passion put to use
In my old griefs, and with my childhood's faith.
I love thee with a love I seemed to lose
With my lost saints, — I love thee with the breath,
Smiles, tears, of all my life! — and, if God choose,
I shall but love thee better after death.

ELIZABETH BARRETT BROWNING (1806–1861)

A Red Red Rose

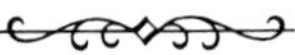

O MY Luve's like a red, red rose,
  That's newly sprung in June;
O my Luve's like the melodie
  That's sweetly play'd in tune. —

As fair art thou, my bonnie lass,
  So deep in luve am I;
And I will love thee still, my Dear,
  Till a' the seas gang dry. —

Till a' the seas gang dry, my Dear,
  And the rocks melt wi' the sun:
I will love thee still, my Dear,
  While the sands o' life shall run. —

And fare thee weel, my only Luve!
  And fare thee weel, a while!
And I will come again, my Luve,
  Tho' it were ten thousand mile!

ROBERT BURNS (1759–1796)

Nicholas Hilliard (1547–1619) *Miniature of a Young Man against a Rose Tree,* Victoria and Albert Museum, London

Henry Ottman (1877–1927) *Woman on a Balcony,* Musée des Beaux Arts, Rouen

She Walks in Beauty

SHE walks in beauty, like the night
Of cloudless climes and starry skies,
And all that's best of dark and bright
Meets in her aspect and her eyes,
Thus mellow'd to that tender light
Which heaven to gaudy day denies.

One shade the more, one ray the less
Had half impair'd the nameless grace
Which waves in every raven tress
Or softly lightens o'er her face,
Where thoughts serenely sweet express
How pure, how dear their dwelling place.

And on that cheek and o'er that brow
So soft, so calm, yet eloquent,
The smiles that win, the tints that glow
But tell of days in goodness spent, —
A mind at peace with all below,
A heart whose love is innocent.

LORD BYRON (1788–1824)

First Love

I NE'ER was struck before that hour
With love so sudden and so sweet,
Her face it bloomed like a sweet flower
And stole my heart away complete.
My face turned pale as deadly pale,
My legs refused to walk away,
And when she looked, what could I ail?
My life and all seemed turned to clay.

And then my blood rushed to my face
And took my eyesight quite away,
The trees and bushes round the place
Seemed midnight at noonday.
I could not see a single thing,
Words from my eyes did start —
They spoke as chords do from the string,
And blood burnt round my heart.

Are flowers the winter's choice?
Is love's bed always snow?
She seemed to hear my silent voice,
Not love's appeals to know.
I never saw so sweet a face
As that I stood before.
My heart has left its dwelling-place
And can return no more.

JOHN CLARE (1793–1864)

Non Sum Qualis Eram Bonae Sub Regno Cynarae

LAST night, ah, yesternight, betwixt her lips and mine
There fell thy shadow, Cynara! thy breath was shed
Upon my soul between the kisses and the wine;
And I was desolate and sick of an old passion,
  Yea, I was desolate and bowed my head:
I have been faithful to thee, Cynara! in my fashion.

All night upon mine heart I felt her warm heart beat,
Night-long within mine arms in love and sleep she lay;
Surely the kisses of her bought red mouth were sweet;
But I was desolate and sick of an old passion,
  When I awoke and found the dawn was gray:
I have been faithful to thee, Cynara! in my fashion.

I have forgot much, Cynara! gone with the wind,
Flung roses, roses riotously with the throng,
Dancing, to put thy pale, lost lilies out of mind;
But I was desolate and sick of an old passion,
  Yea, all the time, because the dance was long:
I have been faithful to thee, Cynara! in my fashion.

I cried for madder music and for stronger wine,
But when the feast is finished and the lamps expire,
Then falls thy shadow, Cynara! the night is thine;
And I am desolate and sick of an old passion,
  Yea, hungry for the lips of my desire:
I have been faithful to thee, Cynara! in my fashion.

ERNEST DOWSON (1867–1900)

Song

1

SYLVIA the fair, in the bloom of fifteen
Felt an innocent warmth, as she lay on the green;
She had heard of a pleasure, and something she guessed
By the towzing and tumbling and touching her breast:
She saw the men eager, but was at a loss,
What they meant by their sighing and kissing so close;
By their praying and whining,
And clasping and twining,
And panting and wishing,
And sighing and kissing,
And sighing and kissing so close.

JOHN DRYDEN (1631–1700)

To the Virgins, To Make Much of Time

GATHER ye rosebuds while ye may,
Old Time is still a-flying:
And this same flower that smiles today
Tomorrow will be dying.

The glorious lamp of heaven, the sun,
The higher he's a-getting,
The sooner will his race be run,
And nearer he's to setting.

That age is best which is the first,
When youth and blood are warmer;
But being spent, the worse, and worst
Times still succeed the former.

Then be not coy, but use your time,
And while ye may, go marry:
For having lost but once your prime,
You may for ever tarry.

ROBERT HERRICK (1591–1674)

One Flesh

LYING apart now, each in a separate bed,
He with a book, keeping the light on late,
She like a girl dreaming of childhood,
All men elsewhere — it is as if they wait
Some new event: the book he holds unread,
Her eyes fixed on the shadows overhead.

Tossed up like flotsam from a former passion,
How cool they lie. They hardly ever touch,
Or if they do it is like a confession
Of having little feeling — or too much.
Chastity faces them, a destination
For which their whole lives were a preparation.

Strangely apart, yet strangely close together,
Silence between them like a thread to hold
And not wind in. And time itself's a feather
Touching them gently. Do they know they're old,
These two who are my father and my mother
Whose fire from which I came, has now grown cold?

ELIZABETH JENNINGS (1926 –)

To Celia

DRINK to me only with thine eyes,
  And I will pledge with mine;
Or leave a kiss but in the cup
  And I'll not look for wine.
The thirst that from the soul doth rise
  Doth ask a drink divine;
But might I of Jove's nectar sup,
  I would not change for thine.

I sent thee late a rosy wreath,
  Not so much honouring thee
As giving it a hope that there
  It could not wither'd be;
But thou thereon didst only breathe
  And sent'st it back to me;
Since when it grows, and smells, I swear,
  Not of itself but thee!

BEN JONSON (1572–1637)

La Belle Dame Sans Merci

'O WHAT can ail thee, knight-at-arms,
  Alone and palely loitering?
The sedge is wither'd from the lake,
  And no birds sing.

O what can ail thee, knight-at-arms,
  So haggard and so woe-begone?
The squirrel's granary is full,
  And the harvest's done.

I see a lily on thy brow
  With anguish moist and fever dew;
And on thy cheek a fading rose
  Fast withereth too.'

'I met a lady in the meads,
  Full beautiful — a faery's child,
Her hair was long, her foot was light,
  And her eyes were wild.

I made a garland for her head,
  And bracelets too, and fragrant zone;
She look'd at me as she did love,
  And made sweet moan.

I set her on my pacing steed
  And nothing else saw all day long,
For sideways would she lean, and sing
  A faery's song.

She found me roots of relish sweet,
  And honey wild and manna dew,
And sure in language strange she said,
  "I love thee true!"

She took me to her elfin grot,
   And there she wept and sigh'd full sore;
And there I shut her wild, wild eyes
   With kisses four.

And there she lullèd me asleep,
   And there I dream'd — Ah! woe betide!
The latest dream I ever dream'd
   On the cold hill's side.

I saw pale kings and princes too,
   Pale warriors, death-pale were they all;
Who cried — "La belle Dame sans Merci
   Hath thee in thrall!"

I saw their starved lips in the gloam
   With horrid warning gapèd wide,
And I awoke and found me here
   On the cold hill's side.

And this is why I sojourn here
   Alone and palely loitering,
Though the sedge is wither'd from the lake,
   And no birds sing.'

John Keats (1795–1821)

The Passionate Shepherd to His Love

COME live with me and be my Love,
And we will all the pleasures prove
That hills and valleys, dale and field,
And all the craggy mountains yield.

There will we sit upon the rocks
And see the shepherds feed their flocks,
By shallow rivers, to whose falls
Melodious birds sing madrigals.

There will I make thee beds of roses
And a thousand fragrant posies,
A cap of flowers, and a kirtle
Embroider'd all with leaves of myrtle.

A gown made of the finest wool,
Which from our pretty lambs we pull,
Fair linéd slippers for the cold,
With buckles of the purest gold.

A belt of straw and ivy buds
With coral clasps and amber studs:
And if these pleasures may thee move,
Come live with me and be my Love.

Thy silver dishes for thy meat
As precious as the gods do eat,
Shall on an ivory table be
Prepared each day for thee and me.

The shepherd swains shall dance and sing
For thy delight each May-morning:
If these delights thy mind may move,
Then live with me and be my Love.

CHRISTOPHER MARLOWE (1564–1593)

To His Coy Mistress

HAD we but world enough, and time,
This coyness, Lady, were no crime.
We would sit down, and think which way
To walk, and pass our long love's day.
Thou by the Indian Ganges' side
Shouldst rubies find: I by the tide
Of Humber would complain. I would
Love you ten years before the Flood:
And you should, if you please, refuse
Till the conversion of the Jews.
My vegetable love should grow
Vaster than empires, and more slow.
An hundred years should go to praise
Thine eyes, and on thy forehead gaze.
Two hundred to adore each breast:
But thirty thousand to the rest.
An age at least to every part,
And the last age should show your heart.
For, Lady, you deserve this state;
Nor would I love at lower rate.
But at my back I always hear
Time's wingèd chariot hurrying near:
And yonder all before us lie
Deserts of vast eternity.
Thy beauty shall no more be found;
Nor, in thy marble vault, shall sound
My echoing song: then worms shall try
That long preserved virginity:
And your quaint honour turn to dust;
And into ashes all my lust.
The grave's a fine and private place,
But none I think do there embrace.
Now therefore, while the youthful hue
Sits on thy skin like morning dew,
And while thy willing soul transpires
At every pore with instant fires,
Now let us sport us while we may;

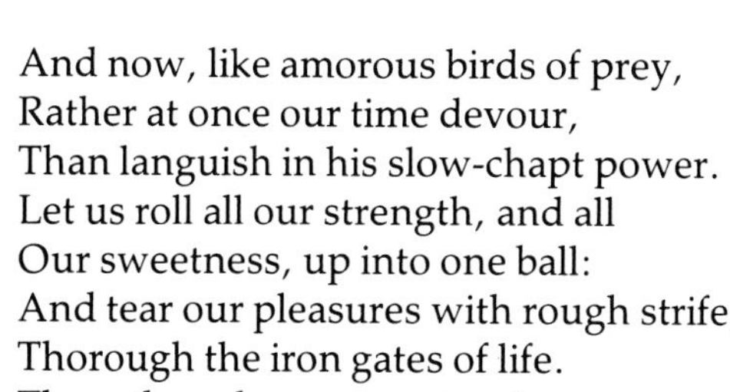

And now, like amorous birds of prey,
Rather at once our time devour,
Than languish in his slow-chapt power.
Let us roll all our strength, and all
Our sweetness, up into one ball:
And tear our pleasures with rough strife,
Thorough the iron gates of life.
Thus, though we cannot make our sun
Stand still, yet we will make him run.

ANDREW MARVELL (1621–1678)

The Shepherdess

SHE walks — the lady of my delight —
  A shepherdess of sheep.
Her flock are thoughts. She keeps them white;
  She guards them from the steep.
She feeds them on the fragrant height,
  And folds them in for sleep.

She roams maternal hills and bright,
  Dark valleys safe and deep.
Into that tender breast at night
  The chastest stars may peep.
She walks — the lady of my delight —
  A shepherdess of sheep.

She holds her little thoughts in sight,
  Though gay they run and leap.
She is so circumspect and right;
  She has her soul to keep.
She walks — the lady of my delight —
  A shepherdess of sheep.

ALICE MEYNELL (1847–1922)

Remember

REMEMBER me when I am gone away,
  Gone far away into the silent land;
  When you can no more hold me by the hand,
Nor I half turn to go yet turning stay.
Remember me when no more day by day
  You tell me of our future that you planned:
  Only remember me; you understand
It will be late to counsel then or pray.
Yet if you should forget me for a while
  And afterwards remember, do not grieve:
  For if the darkness and corruption leave
  A vestige of the thoughts that once I had,
Better by far you should forget and smile
  Than that you should remember and be sad.

CHRISTINA ROSSETTI (1830–1894)

Rose Aylmer

AH, what avails the sceptred race!
  Ah, what the form divine!
What every virtue, every grace!
  Rose Aylmer, all were thine.

Rose Aylmer, whom these wakeful eyes
  May weep, but never see,
A night of memories and sighs
  I consecrate to thee.

WALTER SAVAGE LANDOR (1775–1864)

Shakespeare Sonnets

Sonnet CXVI

Let me not to the marriage of true minds
Admit impediments. Love is not love
Which alters when it alteration finds,
Or bends with the remover to remove:
O, no! it is an ever-fixed mark,
That looks on tempests and is never shaken;
It is the star to every wandering bark,
Whose worth's unknown, although his height be taken.
Love's not Time's fool, though rosy lips and cheeks
Within his bending sickle's compass come;
Love alters not with his brief hours and weeks,
But bears it out even to the edge of doom.
  If this be error and upon me proved,
  I never writ, nor no man ever loved.

Sonnet XVIII

Shall I compare thee to a summer's day?
Thou art more lovely and more temperate:
Rough winds do shake the darling buds of May,
And summer's lease hath all too short a date:
Sometime too hot the eye of heaven shines,
And often is his gold complexion dimm'd;
And every fair from fair sometime declines,
By chance or nature's changing course untrimm'd;
But thy eternal summer shall not fade,
Nor lose possession of that fair thou owest;
Nor shall Death brag thou wander'st in his shade,
When in eternal lines to time thou grow'st:
  So long as men can breathe, or eyes can see,
  So long lives this, and this gives life to thee.

William Shakespeare (1564–1616)

Song of Solomon, Chapter Two

I AM a rose of Sharon,
  a lily of the valleys.

As a lily among brambles,
  so is my love among maidens.

As an apple tree among the trees of the wood,
  so is my beloved among young men.
With great delight I sat in his shadow,
  and his fruit was sweet to my taste.
He brought me to the banqueting house,
  and his banner over me was love.
Sustain me with raisins,
  refresh me with apples;
  for I am sick with love.
O that his left hand were under my head,
  and that his right hand embraced me!
I adjure you, O daughters of Jerusalem,
  by the gazelles or the hinds of the field,
that you stir not up nor awaken love
  until it please.
The voice of my beloved!
  Behold, he comes,
leaping upon the mountains,
  bounding over the hills.
My beloved is like a gazelle,
  or a young stag.
Behold, there he stands
  behind our wall,
gazing in at the windows,
  looking through the lattice.

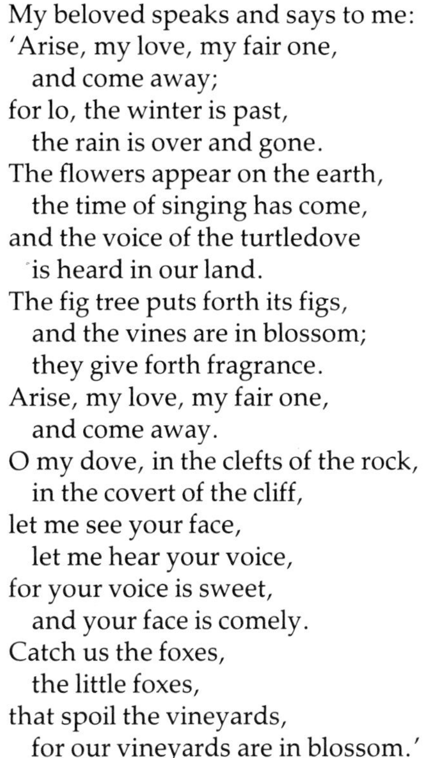

My beloved speaks and says to me:
'Arise, my love, my fair one,
  and come away;
for lo, the winter is past,
  the rain is over and gone.
The flowers appear on the earth,
  the time of singing has come,
and the voice of the turtledove
  is heard in our land.
The fig tree puts forth its figs,
  and the vines are in blossom;
  they give forth fragrance.
Arise, my love, my fair one,
  and come away.
O my dove, in the clefts of the rock,
  in the covert of the cliff,
let me see your face,
  let me hear your voice,
for your voice is sweet,
  and your face is comely.
Catch us the foxes,
  the little foxes,
that spoil the vineyards,
  for our vineyards are in blossom.'

My beloved is mine and I am his,
  he pastures his flock among the lilies.
Until the day breathes
  and the shadows flee,
turn, my beloved, be like a gazelle,
  or a young stag upon rugged mountains.

ATTRIBUTED TO KING SOLOMON

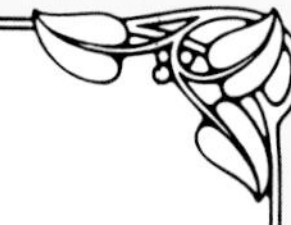

She Was a Phantom of Delight

She was a phantom of delight
When first she gleam'd upon my sight:
A lovely apparition, sent
To be a moment's ornament;
Her eyes as stars of twilight fair;
Like Twilight's, too, her dusky hair;
But all things else about her drawn
From May-time and the cheerful dawn;
A dancing shape, an image gay,
To haunt, to startle, and waylay.

I saw her upon nearer view,
A spirit, yet a woman too!
Her household motions light and free,
And steps of virgin-liberty;
A countenance in which did meet
Sweet records, promises as sweet;
A creature not too bright or good
For human nature's daily food,
For transient sorrows, simple wiles,
Praise, blame, love, kisses, tears, and smiles.

And now I see with eye serene
The very pulse of the machine;
A being breathing thoughtful breath,
A traveller between life and death:
The reason firm, the temperate will,
Endurance, foresight, strength, and skill;
A perfect woman, nobly plann'd
To warn, to comfort, and command;
And yet a Spirit still, and bright
With something of an angel-light.

William Wordsworth (1770–1850)

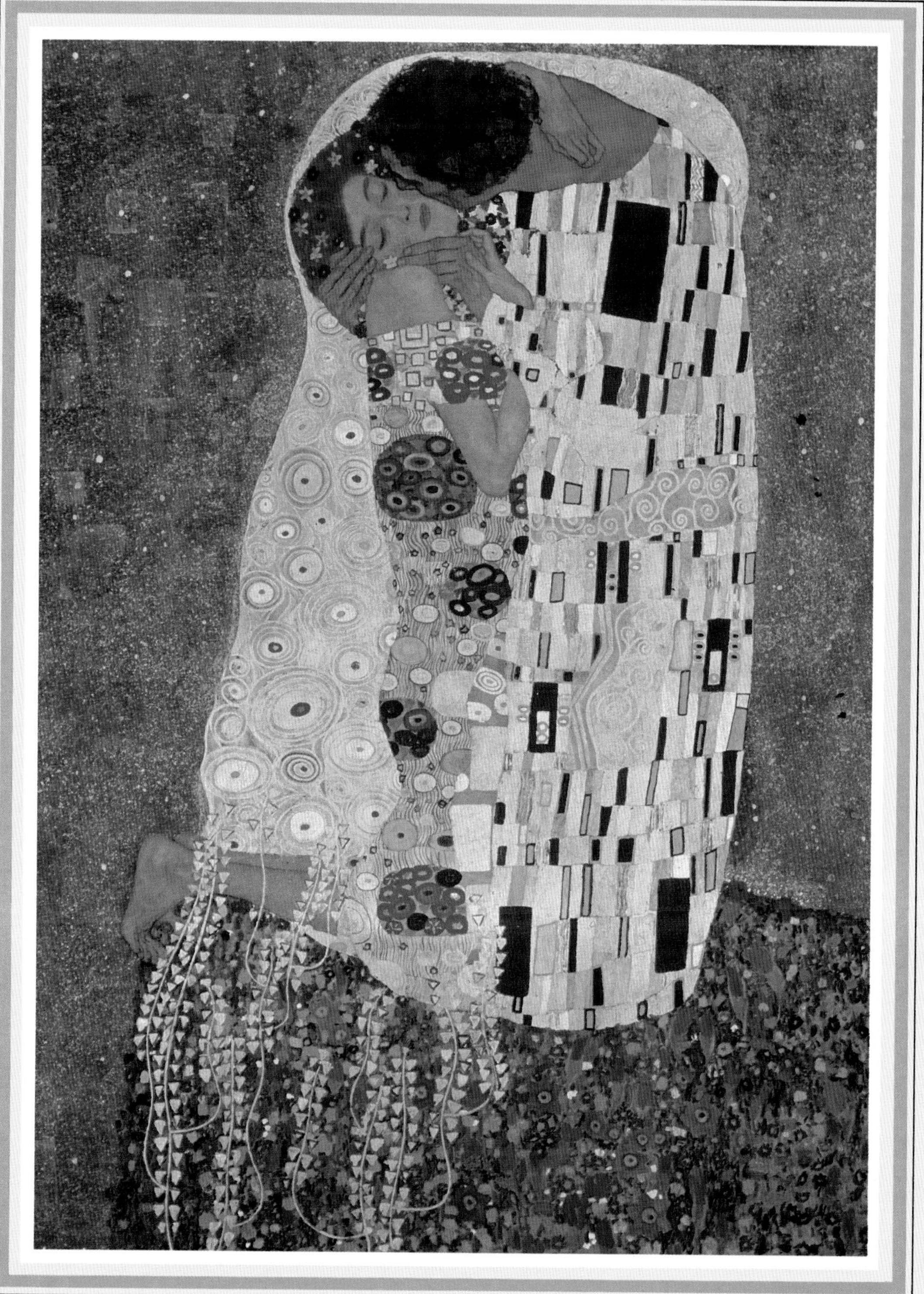

Gustav Klimt (1862–1918) *The Kiss,* Osterreichisches Museum, Vienna

James Jacques Tissot (1826–1902) *Les Adieux,* Bristol City Museum and Art Gallery

When You Are Old

WHEN you are old and grey and full of sleep,
And nodding by the fire, take down this book,
And slowly read, and dream of the soft look
Your eyes had once, and of their shadows deep;

How many loved your moments of glad grace,
And loved your beauty with love false or true,
But one man loved the pilgrim soul in you,
And loved the sorrows of your changing face;

And bending down beside the glowing bars,
Murmur, a little sadly, how Love fled
And paced upon the mountains overhead
And hid his face amid a crowd of stars.

W. B. YEATS (1865–1939)

NOSTALGIA AND REFLECTION

Dover Beach

THE sea is calm to-night.
The tide is full, the moon lies fair
Upon the straits; — on the French coast the light
Gleams and is gone; the cliffs of England stand,
Glimmering and vast, out in the tranquil bay.
Come to the window, sweet is the night-air!
Only, from the long line of spray
Where the sea meets the moon-blanched land,
Listen! you hear the grating roar
Of pebbles which the waves draw back, and fling,
At their return, up the high strand,
Begin, and cease, and then again begin,
With tremulous cadence slow, and bring
The eternal note of sadness in.

Sophocles long ago
Heard it on the AEgæn, and it brought
Into his mind the turbid ebb and flow
Of human misery; we
Find also in the sound a thought,
Hearing it by this distant northern sea.

The Sea of Faith
Was once, too, at the full, and round earth's shore
Lay like the folds of a bright girdle furled.
But now I only hear
Its melancholy, long, withdrawing roar,
Retreating, to the breath
Of the night-wind, down the vast edges drear
And naked shingles of the world.

Ah, love, let us be true
To one another! for the world, which seems
To lie before us like a land of dreams,
So various, so beautiful, so new,
Hath really neither joy, nor love, nor light,
Nor certitude, nor peace, nor help for pain;
And we are here as on a darkling plain
Swept with confused alarms of struggle and flight,
Where ignorant armies clash by night.

MATTHEW ARNOLD (1822–1888)

Almswomen

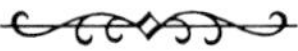

AT Quincey's moat the squandering village ends,
And there in the almshouse dwell the dearest friends
Of all the village, two old dames that cling
As close as any trueloves in the spring.
Long, long ago they passed three-score-and-ten,
And in this doll's-house lived together then;
All things they have in common being so poor,
And their one fear, Death's shadow at the door.
Each sundown makes them mournful, each sunrise
Brings back the brightness in their failing eyes.

How happy go the rich fair-weather days
When on the roadside folk stare in amaze
At such a honeycomb of fruit and flowers
As mellows round their threshold; what long hours
They gloat upon their steepling hollyhocks,
Bee's balsam, feathery southernwood and stocks,
Fiery dragon's-mouths, great mallow leaves
For salves, and lemon-plants in bushy sheaves,
Shagged Esau's-hands with five green finger-tips.
Such old sweet names are ever on their lips.

As pleased as little children where these grow
In cobbled pattens and worn gowns they go,
Proud of their wisdom when on gooseberry shoots
They stuck egg shells to fright from coming fruits
The brisk-billed rascals; scanning still to see
Their neighbour owls saunter from tree to tree,
Or in the hushing half-light mouse the lane
Long-winged and lordly.

But when those hours wane
Indoors they ponder, scared by the harsh storm
Whose pelting saracens on the window swarm,
And listen for the mail to clatter past
And church clock's deep bay withering on the blast;
They feed the fire that flings its freakish light
On pictured kings and queens grotesquely bright,
Platters and pitchers, faded calendars
And graceful hourglass trim with lavenders.

Many a time they kiss and cry and pray
That both be summoned in the selfsame day,
And wiseman linnet tinkling in his cage
End too with them the friendship of old age,
And all together leave their treasured room
Some bell-like evening when the May's in bloom.

Edmund Blunden (1896–1974)

The Old Vicarage, Grantchester

(Café des Westens, Berlin, May 1912)

JUST now the lilac is in bloom,
All before my little room;
And in my flower-beds, I think,
Smile the carnation and the pink;
And down the borders, well I know,
The poppy and the pansy blow . . .
Oh! there the chestnuts, summer through,
Beside the river make for you
A tunnel of green gloom, and sleep
Deeply above; and green and deep
The stream mysterious glides beneath,
Green as a dream and deep as death.
— Oh, damn! I know it! and I know
How the May fields all golden show,
And when the day is young and sweet,
Gild gloriously the bare feet
That run to bathe . . .
Du lieber Gott!

Here am I, sweating, sick, and hot,
And there the shadowed waters fresh
Lean up to embrace the naked flesh.
Temperamentvoll German Jews
Drink beer around; — and *there* the dews
Are soft beneath a morn of gold.
Here tulips bloom as they are told;
Unkempt about those hedges blows
An English unofficial rose;
And there the unregulated sun
Slopes down to rest when day is done,
And wakes a vague unpunctual star,
A slippered Hesper; and there are
Meads towards Haslingfield and Coton
Where *das Betreten's* not *verboten*.

εἴθε γενοίμην . . . would I were
In Grantchester, in Grantchester! —
Some, it may be, can get in touch
With Nature there, or Earth, or such.
And clever modern men have seen
A Faun a-peeping through the green,
And felt the Classics were not dead,
To glimpse a Naiad's reedy head,
Or hear the Goat-foot piping low: . . .
But these are things I do not know.
I only know that you may lie
Day-long and watch the Cambridge sky,
And, flower-lulled in sleepy grass,
Hear the cool lapse of hours pass,
Until the centuries blend and blur
In Grantchester, in Grantchester . . .
Still in the dawnlit waters cool
His ghostly Lordship swims his pool,
And tries the strokes, essays the tricks,
Long learnt on Hellespont, or Styx.
Dan Chaucer hears his river still
Chatter beneath a phantom mill.
Tennyson notes, with studious eye,
How Cambridge waters hurry by . . .
And in that garden, black and white,
Creep whispers through the grass all night;
And spectral dance, before the dawn,
A hundred Vicars down the lawn;
Curates, long dust, will come and go
On lissom, clerical, printless toe;
And oft between the boughs is seen
The sly shade of a Rural Dean . . .
Till, at a shiver in the skies,
Vanishing with Satanic cries,
The prim ecclesiastic rout
Leaves but a startled sleeper-out,
Grey heavens, the first bird's drowsy calls,
The falling house that never falls.

God! I will pack, and take a train,
And get me to England once again!
For England's the one land, I know,
Where men with Splendid Hearts may go;
And Cambridgeshire, of all England,
The shire for Men who Understand;
And of *that* district I prefer
The lovely hamlet Grantchester.
For Cambridge people rarely smile,
Being urban, squat, and packed with guile;
And Royston men in the far South
Are black and fierce and strange of mouth;
At Over they fling oaths at one,
And worse than oaths at Trumpington,
And Ditton girls are mean and dirty,
And there's none in Harston under thirty,
And folks in Shelford and those parts
Have twisted lips and twisted hearts,
And Barton men make Cockney rhymes,
And Coton's full of nameless crimes,
And things are done you'd not believe
At Madingley, on Christmas Eve.
Strong men have run for miles and miles,
When one from Cherry Hinton smiles;
Strong men have blanched, and shot their wives,
Rather than send them to St. Ives;
Strong men have cried like babes, bydam,
To hear what happened at Babraham.
But Grantchester! ah, Grantchester!
There's peace and holy quiet there,
Great clouds along pacific skies,
And men and women with straight eyes,
Lithe children lovelier than a dream,
A bosky wood, a slumbrous stream,
And little kindly winds that creep
Round twilight corners, half asleep.
In Grantchester their skins are white;
They bathe by day, they bathe by night;
The women there do all they ought;
The men observe the Rules of Thought.

They love the Good; they worship Truth;
They laugh uproariously in youth;
(And when they get to feeling old,
They up and shoot themselves, I'm told) . . .
  Ah God! to see the branches stir
Across the moon at Grantchester!
To smell the thrilling-sweet and rotten
Unforgettable, unforgotten
River-smell, and hear the breeze
Sobbing in the little trees.
Say, do the elm-clumps greatly stand
Still guardians of that holy land?
The chestnuts shade, in reverend dream,
The yet unacademic stream?
Is dawn a secret shy and cold
Anadyomene, silver-gold?
And sunset still a golden sea
From Haslingfield to Madingley?
And after, ere the night is born,
Do hares come out about the corn?
Oh, is the water sweet and cool,
Gentle and brown, above the pool?
And laughs the immortal river still
Under the mill, under the mill?
Say, is there Beauty yet to find?
And Certainty? and Quiet kind?
Deep meadows yet, for to forget
The lies, and truths, and pain? . . . oh! yet
Stands the Church clock at ten to three?
And is there honey still for tea?

RUPERT BROOKE (1887–1915)

Home-Thoughts, from Abroad

OH, TO be in England
Now that April's there,
And whoever wakes in England
Sees, some morning, unaware,
That the lowest boughs and the brushwood sheaf
Round the elm-tree bole are in tiny leaf,
While the chaffinch sings on the orchard bough
In England — now!
And after April, when May follows,
And the whitethroat builds, and all the swallows!
Hark, where my blossomed pear-tree in the hedge
Leans to the field and scatters on the clover
Blossoms and dewdrops — at the bent spray's edge —
That's the wise thrush; he sings each song twice over,
Lest you should think he never could recapture
The first fine careless rapture!
And though the fields look rough with hoary dew,
All will be gay when noontide wakes anew
The buttercups, the little children's dower
— Far brighter than this gaudy melon-flower!

ROBERT BROWNING (1812–1889)

Heraclitus

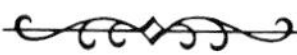

THEY told me, Heraclitus, they told me you were dead,
They brought me bitter news to hear and bitter tears to shed.
I wept as I remember'd how often you and I
Had tired the sun with talking and sent him down the sky.

And now that thou art lying, my dear old Carian guest,
A handful of grey ashes, long, long ago at rest,
Still are thy pleasant voices, thy nightingales, awake;
For Death, he taketh all away, but them he cannot take.

WILLIAM CORY (1823–1892)

Leisure

WHAT is this life if, full of care,
We have no time to stand and stare.

No time to stand beneath the boughs
And stare as long as sheep or cows.

No time to see, when woods we pass,
Where squirrels hide their nuts in grass.

No time to see, in broad daylight,
Streams full of stars, like skies at night.

No time to turn at Beauty's glance,
And watch her feet, how they can dance.

No time to wait till her mouth can
Enrich that smile her eyes began.

A poor life this if, full of care,
We have no time to stand and stare.

W. H. DAVIES (1871–1940)

Elegy Written in a Country Churchyard

THE curfew tolls the knell of parting day,
The lowing herd wind slowly o'er the lea,
The ploughman homeward plods his weary way,
And leaves the world to darkness and to me.

Now fades the glimmering landscape on the sight,
And all the air a solemn stillness holds,
Save where the beetle wheels his droning flight,
And drowsy tinklings lull the distant folds;

Save that from yonder ivy-mantled tower
The moping owl does to the moon complain
Of such as, wandering near her secret bower,
Molest her ancient solitary reign.

Beneath those rugged elms, that yew-tree's shade,
Where heaves the turf in many a mouldering heap,
Each in his narrow cell for ever laid,
The rude forefathers of the hamlet sleep.

The breezy call of incense-breathing morn,
The swallow twittering from the straw-built shed,
The cock's shrill clarion or the echoing horn,
No more shall rouse them from their lowly bed.

For them no more the blazing hearth shall burn,
Or busy housewife ply her evening care:
No children run to lisp their sire's return,
Or climb his knees the envied kiss to share.

Oft did the harvest to their sickle yield,
Their furrow oft the stubborn glebe has broke;
How jocund did they drive their team afield!
How bowed the woods beneath their sturdy stroke!

Let not Ambition mock their useful toil,
Their homely joys and destiny obscure;
Nor Grandeur hear, with a disdainful smile,
The short and simple annals of the poor.

The boast of heraldry, the pomp of power,
And all that beauty, all that wealth e'er gave,
Awaits alike the inevitable hour.
The paths of glory lead but to the grave.

Nor you, ye Proud, impute to these the fault,
If Memory o'er their tomb no trophies raise,
Where through the long-drawn aisle and fretted vault
The pealing anthem swells the note of praise.

Can storied urn or animated bust
Back to its mansion call the fleeting breath?
Can Honour's voice provoke the silent dust,
Or Flattery soothe the dull cold ear of Death?

Perhaps in this neglected spot is laid
Some heart once pregnant with celestial fire;
Hands that the rod of empire might have swayed,
Or waked to ecstasy the living lyre.

But Knowledge to their eyes her ample page
Rich with the spoils of time did ne'er unroll;
Chill Penury repressed their noble rage,
And froze the genial current of the soul.

Full many a gem of purest ray serene
The dark unfathomed caves of ocean bear:
Full many a flower is born to blush unseen,
And waste its sweetness on the desert air.

Some village-Hampden that with dauntless breast
The little tyrant of his fields withstood;
Some mute inglorious Milton here may rest,
Some Cromwell guiltless of his country's blood.

The applause of listening senates to command,
The threats of pain and ruin to despise,
To scatter plenty o'er a smiling land,
And read their history in a nation's eyes,

Their lot forbade: nor circumscribed alone
Their growing virtues, but their crimes confined;
Forbade to wade through slaughter to a throne,
And shut the gates of mercy on mankind,

The struggling pangs of conscious truth to hide,
To quench the blushes of ingenuous shame,
Or heap the shrine of Luxury and Pride
With incense kindled at the Muse's flame.

Far from the madding crowd's ignoble strife
Their sober wishes never learned to stray;
Along the cool sequestered vale of life
They kept the noiseless tenor of their way.

Yet even these bones from insult to protect
Some frail memorial still erected nigh,
With uncouth rhymes and shapeless sculpture decked,
Implores the passing tribute of a sigh.

Their name, their years, spelt by the unlettered muse,
The place of fame and elegy supply:
And many a holy text around she strews,
That teach the rustic moralist to die.

For who to dumb Forgetfulness a prey,
This pleasing anxious being e'er resigned,
Left the warm precincts of the cheerful day,
Nor cast one longing lingering look behind?

On some fond breast the parting soul relies,
Some pious drops the closing eye requires;
Even from the tomb the voice of Nature cries,
Even in our ashes live their wonted fires.

For thee who, mindful of the unhonoured dead,
Dost in these lines their artless tale relate;
If chance, by lonely Contemplation led,
Some kindred spirit shall inquire thy fate.

Haply some hoary-headed swain may say,
'Oft have we seen him at the peep of dawn
Brushing with hasty steps the dews away
To meet the sun upon the upland lawn.

'There at the foot of yonder nodding beech
That wreathes its old fantastic roots so high,
His listless length at noontide would he stretch,
And pore upon the brook that babbles by.

'Hard by yon wood, now smiling as in scorn,
Muttering his wayward fancies he would rove,
Now drooping, woeful wan, like one forlorn,
Or crazed with care, or crossed in hopeless love.

'One morn I missed him on the customed hill,
Along the heath and near his favourite tree;
Another came; nor yet beside the rill,
Nor up the lawn, nor at the wood was he;

'The next with dirges due in sad array
Slow through the church-way path we saw him borne.
Approach and read (for thou canst read) the lay,
Graved on the stone beneath yon aged thorn.'

THE EPITAPH

Here rests his head upon the lap of earth
A youth to Fortune and to Fame unknown.
Fair Science frowned not on his humble birth,
And Melancholy marked him for her own.

Large was his bounty and his soul sincere,
Heaven did a recompense as largely send:
He gave to Misery all he had, a tear,
He gained from Heaven ('twas all he wished) a friend.

No farther seek his merits to disclose,
Or draw his frailties from their dread abode,
(There they alike in trembling hope repose)
The bosom of his Father and his God.

THOMAS GRAY (1716–1771)

Paul Signac (1863–1945) *The Island at Lucas near Les Andelys,* Christie's, London

George Vicat Cole (1833–1893) *Landscape – Harvest Time* (detail), City of Bristol Museum and Art Gallery

Felix Randal

FELIX RANDAL the farrier, O he is dead then? my duty all ended,
Who have watched his mould of man, big-boned and hardy-handsome
Pining, pining, till time when reason rambled in it and some
Fatal four disorders, fleshed there, all contended?

Sickness broke him. Impatient he cursed at first, but mended
Being anointed and all; though a heavenlier heart began some
Months earlier, since I had our sweet reprieve and ransom
Tendered to him. Ah well, God rest him all road ever he offended!

This seeing the sick endears them to us, us too it endears.
My tongue had taught thee comfort, touch had quenched thy tears,
Thy tears that touched my heart, child, Felix, poor Felix Randal;

How far from then forethought of, all thy more boisterous years,
When thou at the random grim forge, powerful amidst peers,
Didst fettle for the great grey drayhorse his bright and battering sandal!

GERARD MANLEY HOPKINS (1844–1889)

Fancy's Knell

WHEN lads were home from labour
At Abdon under Clee,
A man would call his neighbour
And both would send for me.
And where the light in lances
Across the mead was laid,
There to the dances
I fetched my flute and played.

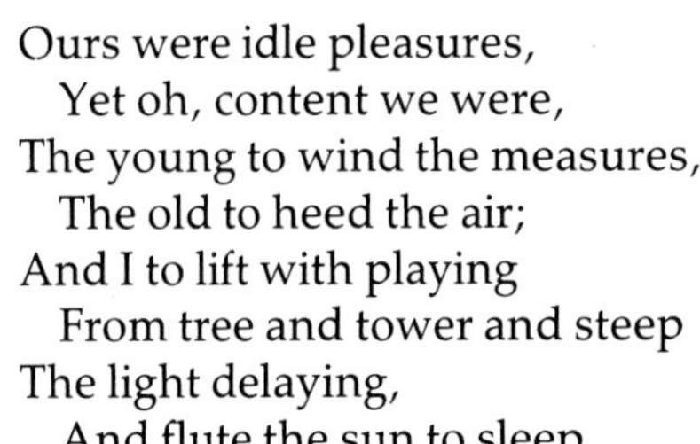

Ours were idle pleasures,
  Yet oh, content we were,
The young to wind the measures,
  The old to heed the air;
And I to lift with playing
  From tree and tower and steep
The light delaying,
  And flute the sun to sleep.

The youth toward his fancy
  Would turn his brow of tan,
And Tom would pair with Nancy
  And Dick step off with Fan;
The girl would lift her glances
  To his, and both be mute:
Well went the dances
  At evening to the flute.

Wenlock Edge was umbered,
  And bright was Abdon Burf,
And warm between them slumbered
  The smooth green miles of turf;
Until from grass and clover
  The upshot beam would fade,
And England over
  Advanced the lofty shade.

The lofty shade advances,
  I fetch my flute and play:
Come, lads, and learn the dances
  And praise the tune to-day.
To-morrow, more's the pity,
  Away we both must hie,
To air the ditty,
  And to earth I.

A. E. HOUSMAN (1859–1936)

Cities and Thrones and Powers

Cities and Thrones and Powers
  Stand in Time's eye,
Almost as long as flowers,
  Which daily die:
But, as new buds put forth
  To glad new men,
Out of the spent and unconsidered Earth
  The Cities rise again.

This season's Daffodil,
  She never hears
What change, what chance, what chill,
  Cut down last year's;
But with bold countenance,
  And knowledge small,
Esteems her seven days' continuance
  To be perpetual.

So Time that is o'er-kind
  To all that be,
Ordains us e'en as blind,
  As bold as she:
That in our very death,
  And burial sure,
Shadow to shadow, well persuaded, saith,
'See how our works endure!'

Rudyard Kipling (1865–1936)

April Rise

If Ever I saw blessing in the air
   I see it now in this still early day
Where lemon-green the vaporous morning drips
   Wet sunlight on the powder of my eye.

Blown bubble-film of blue, the sky wraps round
   Weeds of warm light whose every root and rod
Splutters with soapy green, and all the world
   Sweats with the bead of summer in its bud.

If ever I heard blessing it is there
   Where birds in trees that shoals and shadows are
Splash with their hidden wings and drops of sound
   Break on my ears their crests of throbbing air.

Pure in the haze the emerald sun dilates,
   The lips of sparrows milk the mossy stones,
While white as water by the lake a girl
   Swims her green hand among the gathered swans.

Now, as the almond burns its smoking wick,
   Dropping small flames to light the candled grass;
Now, as my low blood scales its second chance,
   If ever world were blessed, now it is.

Laurie Lee (1914 –)

The Light of Other Days

Oft in the stilly night
   Ere slumber's chain has bound me,
Fond Memory brings the light
   Of other days around me:
      The smiles, the tears
      Of boyhood's years,
   The words of love then spoken;
      The eyes that shone,
      Now dimm'd and gone,
   The cheerful hearts now broken!
Thus in the stilly night
   Ere slumber's chain has bound me,
Sad Memory brings the light
   Of other days around me.

When I remember all
   The friends so link'd together
I've seen around me fall
   Like leaves in wintry weather,
      I feel like one
      Who treads alone
   Some banquet-hall deserted,
      Whose lights are fled
      Whose garlands dead,
   And all but he departed!
Thus in the stilly night
   Ere slumber's chain has bound me,
Sad Memory brings the light
   Of other days around me.

Thomas Moore (1779–1852)

The Toys

MY little Son, who looked from thoughtful eyes
And moved and spoke in quiet grown-up wise,
Having my law the seventh time disobeyed,
I struck him, and dismissed
With hard words and unkissed,
His Mother, who was patient, being dead.
Then, fearing lest his grief should hinder sleep,
I visited his bed,
But found him slumbering deep,
With darkened eyelids, and their lashes yet
From his late sobbing wet.
And I, with moan,
Kissing away his tears, left others of my own;
For, on a table drawn beside his head,
He had put, within his reach,
A box of counters and a red-veined stone,
A piece of glass abraded by the beach,
And six or seven shells,
A bottle with bluebells
And two French copper coins, ranged there with careful art,
To comfort his sad heart.

So when that night I prayed
To God, I wept, and said:
Ah, when at last we lie with trancèd breath,
Not vexing Thee in death,
And Thou rememberest of what toys
We made our joys,
How weakly understood,
Thy great commanded good,
Then, fatherly not less
Than I whom Thou hast moulded from the clay,
Thou'lt leave Thy wrath, and say,
'I will be sorry for their childishness.'

COVENTRY PATMORE (1823–1896)

A Farewell to Arms

MY golden locks Time hath to silver turn'd;
  O Time too swift, O swiftness never ceasing!
My youth 'gainst age, and age 'gainst time, hath spurn'd,
  But spurn'd in vain; youth waneth by increasing:
Beauty, strength, youth, are flowers but fading seen;
Duty, faith, love, are roots, and ever green.

My helmet now shall make an hive for bees,
  And lover's sonnets turn to holy psalms;
A man-at-arms must now serve on his knees,
  And feed on prayers, which are old age his alms:
But though from court to cottage I depart,
My saint is sure of my unspotted heart.

And when I saddest sit in homely cell,
  I'll teach my swains this carol for a song, —
'Blest be the hearts that wish my sovereign well,
  Curst be the souls that think her any wrong!'
Goddess, allow this aged man his right
To be your beadsman now that was your knight.

GEORGE PEELE (1558–1597)

Ozymandias of Egypt

I MET a traveller from an antique land
Who said: Two vast and trunkless legs of stone
Stand in the desert. Near them on the sand,
Half sunk, a shatter'd visage lies, whose frown
And wrinkled lip and sneer of cold command
Tell that its sculptor well those passions read
Which yet survive, stamp'd on these lifeless things,
The hand that mock'd them and the heart that fed;
And on the pedestal these words appear:
'My name is Ozymandias, king of kings:
Look on my works, ye Mighty, and despair!'
Nothing beside remains. Round the decay
Of that colossal wreck, boundless and bare,
The lone and level sands stretch far away.

PERCY BYSSHE SHELLEY (1792–1822)

Brown Penny

I whispered, 'I am too young,'
And then, 'I am old enough';
Wherefore I threw a penny
To find out if I might love.
'Go and love, go and love, young man,
If the lady be young and fair.'
Ah, penny, brown penny, brown penny,
I am looped in the loops of her hair.

O love is the crooked thing,
There is nobody wise enough
To find out all that is in it,
For he would be thinking of love
Till the stars had run away
And the shadows eaten the moon.
Ah, penny, brown penny, brown penny,
One cannot begin it too soon.

W. B. YEATS (1865–1939)

LYRICAL

We'll Go No More A-Roving

So we'll go no more a-roving
  So late into the night,
Though the heart be still as loving,
  And the moon be still as bright.

For the sword outwears its sheath,
  And the soul wears out the breast,
And the heart must pause to breathe,
  And love itself have rest.

Though the night was made for loving,
  And the day returns too soon,
Yet we'll go no more a-roving
  By the light of the moon.

LORD BYRON (1788–1824)

Kubla Khan

In Xanadu did Kubla Khan
A stately pleasure-dome decree:
Where Alph, the sacred river, ran
Through caverns measureless to man
  Down to a sunless sea.
So twice five miles of fertile ground
With walls and towers were girdled round:
And here were gardens bright with sinuous rills,
Where blossomed many an incense-bearing tree;
And here were forests ancient as the hills,
Enfolding sunny spots of greenery.

But oh! that deep romantic chasm which slanted
Down the green hill athwart a cedarn cover!
A savage place! as holy and enchanted
As e'er beneath a waning moon was haunted
By woman wailing for her demon-lover!

And from this chasm, with ceaseless turmoil seething
As if this earth in fast thick pants were breathing,
A mighty fountain momently was forced:
Amid whose swift half-intermitted burst
Huge fragments vaulted like rebounding hail
Or chaffy grain beneath the thresher's flail:
And mid these dancing rocks at once and ever
It flung up momently the sacred river.
Five miles meandering with a mazy motion
Through wood and dale the sacred river ran,
Then reached the caverns measureless to man,
And sank in tumult to a lifeless ocean:
And 'mid this tumult Kubla heard from far
Ancestral voices prophesying war!

The shadow of the dome of pleasure
Floated midway on the waves;
Where was heard the mingled measure
From the fountain and the caves.
It was a miracle of rare device,
A sunny pleasure-dome with caves of ice!

A damsel with a dulcimer
In a vision once I saw:
It was an Abyssinian maid,
And on her dulcimer she played,
Singing of Mount Abora.
Could I revive within me
Her symphony and song,
To such a deep delight 'twould win me,
That with music loud and long,
I would build that dome in air,
That sunny dome! those caves of ice!
And all who heard should see them there,
And all should cry, Beware! Beware!
His flashing eyes, his floating hair!
Weave a circle round him thrice,
And close your eyes with holy dread,
For he on honey-dew hath fed,
And drunk the milk of Paradise.

Samuel Taylor Coleridge (1772–1834)

A Fancy from Fontenelle

'De mémoires de Roses on n'a point vu mourir le Jardinier.'

THE Rose in the garden slipped her bud,
And she laughed in the pride of her youthful blood,
As she thought of the Gardener standing by —
'He is old, — so old! And he soon must die!'

The full Rose waxed in the warm June air,
And she spread and spread till her heart lay bare;
And she laughed once more as she heard his tread —
'He is older now! He will soon be dead!'

But the breeze of the morning blew, and found
That the leaves of the blown Rose strewed the ground;
And he came at noon, that Gardener old,
And he raked them gently under the mould.

And I wove the thing to a random rhyme,
For the Rose is Beauty, the Gardener, Time.

AUSTIN DOBSON (1840–1921)

Song

GO, AND catch a falling star,
  Get with child a mandrake root,
Tell me, where all past years are,
  Or who cleft the Devil's foot,
Teach me to hear mermaids singing,
  Or to keep off envy's stinging,
    And find
    What wind
Serves to advance an honest mind.

If thou be'st born to strange sights,
  Things invisible to see,
Ride ten thousand days and nights,
  Till age snow white hairs on thee,
Thou, when thou return'st, wilt tell me
All strange wonders that befell thee,
    And swear
    No where
Lives a woman true, and fair.

If thou find'st one, let me know,
  Such a pilgrimage were sweet;
Yet do not, I would not go,
  Though at next door we might meet,
Though she were true, when you met her,
And last, till you write your letter,
    Yet she
    Will be
False, ere I come, to two, or three.

JOHN DONNE (1572–1631)

The Old Ships

I HAVE seen old ships sail like swans asleep
Beyond the village which men still call Tyre,
With leaden age o'ercargoed, dipping deep
For Famagusta and the hidden sun
That rings black Cyprus with a lake of fire;
And all those ships were certainly so old
Who knows how oft with squat and noisy gun,
Questing brown slaves or Syrian oranges,
The pirate Genoese
Hell-raked them till they rolled
Blood, water, fruit and corpses up the hold.
But now through friendly seas they softly run,
Painted the mid-sea blue or shore-sea green,
Still patterned with the vine and grapes in gold.

But I have seen,
Pointing her shapely shadows from the dawn
And image tumbled on a rose-swept bay,
A drowsy ship of some yet older day;
And, wonder's breath indrawn,
Thought I — who knows — who knows — but in that same
(Fished up beyond Aeaea, patched up new
— Stern painted brighter blue —)
That talkative, bald-headed seaman came
(Twelve patient comrades sweating at the oar)
From Troy's doom-crimson shore,
And with great lies about his wooden horse
Set the crew laughing, and forgot his course.

It was so old a ship — who knows, who knows?
— And yet so beautiful, I watched in vain
To see the mast burst open with a rose,
And the whole deck put on its leaves again.

JAMES ELROY FLECKER (1884–1915)

Pan With Us

PAN came out of the woods one day, —
His skin and his hair and his eyes were grey,
The grey of the moss of walls were they, —
  And stood in the sun and looked his fill
  At wooded valley and wooded hill.

He stood in the zephyr, pipes in hand,
On a height of naked pasture land;
In all the country he did command
  He saw no smoke and he saw no roof.
  That was well! and he stamped a hoof.

His heart knew peace, for none came here
To this lean feeding save once a year
Someone to salt the half-wild steer,
  Or homespun children with clicking pails
  Who see so little they tell no tales.

He tossed his pipes, too hard to teach
A new-world song, far out of reach,
For a sylvan sign that the blue jay's screech
  And the whimper of hawks beside the sun
  Were music enough for him, for one.

Times were changed from what they were:
Such pipes kept less of power to stir
The fruited bough of the juniper
  And the fragile bluets clustered there
  Than the merest aimless breath of air.

They were pipes of pagan mirth,
And the world had found new terms of worth.
He laid him down on the sun-burned earth
  And ravelled a flower and looked away —
  Play? Play? — What should he play?

ROBERT FROST (1874–1963)

Edmund George Gosse (1834–1909) *Avenue, Evelyn Wood,* Private Collection

Sir Lawrence Alma-Tadema (1836–1912) *At the Window,* Christopher Wood Gallery, London

The Poetry of Dress

[*Delight in Disorder*]

A SWEET disorder in the dress
Kindles in clothes a wantonness:—
A lawn about the shoulders thrown
Into a fine distractión, —
An erring lace, which here and there
Enthrals the crimson stomacher, —
A cuff neglectful, and thereby
Ribbands to flow confusedly, —
A winning wave, deserving note,
In the tempestuous petticoat, —
A careless shoe-string, in whose tie
I see a wild civility, —
Do more bewitch me, than when art
Is too precise in every part.

[*Upon Julia's Clothes*]

WHENAS in silks my Julia goes
Then, then (methinks) how sweetly flows
That liquefaction of her clothes.

Next, when I cast mine eyes and see
That brave vibration each way free;
O how that glittering taketh me!

ROBERT HERRICK (1591–1674)

Ruth

SHE stood breast high amid the corn,
Clasp'd by the golden light of morn,
Like the sweetheart of the sun,
Who many a glowing kiss had won.

On her cheek an autumn flush,
Deeply ripened; — such a blush
In the midst of brown was born,
Like red poppies grown with corn.

Round her eyes her tresses fell,
Which were blackest none could tell,
But long lashes veil'd a light
That had else been all too bright.

And her hat, with shady brim,
Made her tressy forehead dim; —
Thus she stood amid the stooks,
Praising God with sweetest looks:—

Sure, I said, Heav'n did not mean,
Where I reap thou shouldst but glean,
Lay thy sheaf adown and come,
Share my harvest and my home.

THOMAS HOOD (1799–1845)

Ode

WE are the music makers,
  And we are the dreamers of dreams,
Wandering by lone sea-breakers,
  And sitting by desolate streams; —
World-losers and world-forsakers,
  On whom the pale moon gleams:
Yet we are the movers and shakers
  Of the world for ever, it seems.

With wonderful deathless ditties
We build up the world's great cities,
  And out of a fabulous story
  We fashion an empire's glory:
One man with a dream, at pleasure,
  Shall go forth and conquer a crown;
And three with a new song's measure
  Can trample a kingdom down.

We, in the ages lying
  In the buried past of the earth,
Built Nineveh with our sighing,
  And Babel itself in our mirth;
And o'erthrew them with prophesying
  To the old of the new world's worth;
For each age is a dream that is dying,
  Or one that is coming to birth.

ARTHUR O'SHAUGHNESSY (1844–1881)

In the Poppy Field

MAD Patsy said, he said to me,
That every morning he could see
An angel walking on the sky;
Across the sunny skies of morn
He threw great handfuls far and nigh
Of poppy seed among the corn;
And then, he said, the angels run
To see the poppies in the sun.

A poppy is a devil weed,
I said to him — he disagreed;
He said the devil had no hand
In spreading flowers tall and fair
Through corn and rye and meadow land,
By garth and barrow everywhere:
The devil has not any flower,
But only money in his power.

And then he stretched out in the sun
And rolled upon his back for fun:
He kicked his legs and roared for joy
Because the sun was shining down:
He said he was a little boy
And would not work for any clown:
He ran and laughed behind a bee,
And danced for very ecstasy.

JAMES STEPHENS (1882–1950)

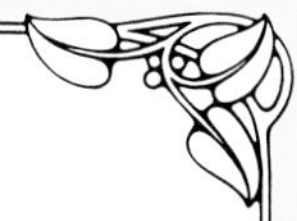

And Death Shall Have No Dominion

And death shall have no dominion.
Dead men naked they shall be one
With the man in the wind and the west moon;
When their bones are picked clean and the clean bones gone,
They shall have stars at elbow and foot;
Though they go mad they shall be sane,
Though they sink through the sea they shall rise again;
Though lovers be lost love shall not;
And death shall have no dominion.

And death shall have no dominion.
Under the windings of the sea
They lying long shall not die windily;
Twisting on racks when sinews give way,
Strapped to a wheel, yet they shall not break;
Faith in their hands shall snap in two,
And the unicorn evils run them through;
Split all ends up they shan't crack;
And death shall have no dominion.

And death shall have no dominion.
No more may gulls cry at their ears
Or waves break loud on the seashores;
Where blew a flower may a flower no more
Lif its head to the blows of the rain;
Though they be mad and dead as nails,
Heads of the characters hammer through daisies;
Break in the sun till the sun breaks down,
And death shall have no dominion.

DYLAN THOMAS (1914–1953)

SPIRITUAL

The Pilgrim

WHO would true valour see,
Let him come hither;
One here will constant be,
Come wind, come weather.
There's no discouragement
Shall make him once relent
His first avowed intent
To be a Pilgrim.

Who so beset him round
With dismal stories
Do but themselves confound;
His strength the more is.
No lion can him fright,
He'll with a giant fight,
But he will have a right
To be a Pilgrim.

Hobgoblin nor foul fiend
Can daunt his spirit:
He knows he at the end
Shall life inherit.
Then fancies fly away,
He'll fear not what men say,
He'll labour night and day
To be a Pilgrim.

JOHN BUNYAN (1628–1688)

Lord of the Dance

I DANCED in the morning
When the world was begun,
And I danced in the moon
And the stars and the sun
And I came down from heaven
And I danced on the earth —
At Bethlehem I had my birth.

Dance then wherever you may be;
I am the Lord of the Dance, said he,
I'll lead you all, wherever you may be,
I will lead you all in the Dance, said he.

I danced for the scribe
And the pharisee,
But they would not dance
And they couldn't follow me;
I danced for the fishermen,
For James and John —
They came with me
And the dance went on.

I danced on the Sabbath
And I cured the lame;
The holy people
Said it was a shame;
They whipped and they stripped
And they hung me high,
And they left me there
On a Cross to die.

I danced on a Friday
When the sky turned black —
It's hard to dance
With the devil on your back;
They buried my body
And they thought I'd gone —
But I am the dance
And I still go on.

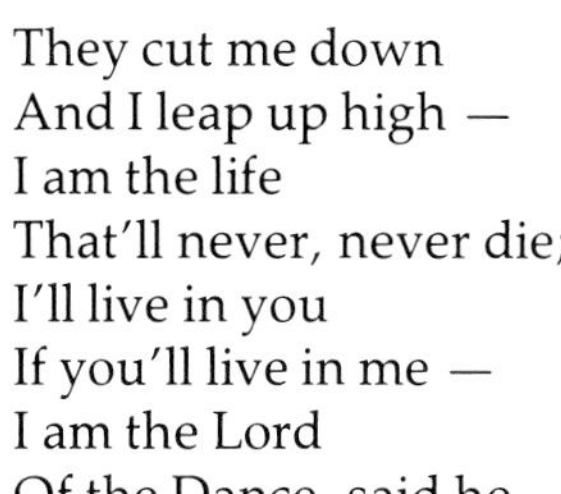

They cut me down
And I leap up high —
I am the life
That'll never, never die;
I'll live in you
If you'll live in me —
I am the Lord
Of the Dance, said he.

Dance then wherever you may be;
I am the Lord of the Dance, said he,
I'll lead you all, wherever you may be,
I will lead you all in the Dance, said he.

Sydney Carter (1915–   )

Brahma

If the red slayer think he slays,
  Or if the slain think he is slain,
They know not well the subtle ways
  I keep, and pass, and turn again.

Far or forgot to me is near;
  Shadow and sunlight are the same;
The vanished gods to me appear;
  And one to me are shame and fame.

They reckon ill who leave me out;
  When me they fly, I am the wings;
I am the doubter and the doubt,
  And I the hymn the Brahmin sings.

The strong gods pine for my abode,
  And pine in vain the sacred Seven;
But thou, meek lover of the good!
  Find me, and turn thy back on heaven.

Ralph Waldo Emerson (1803–1882)

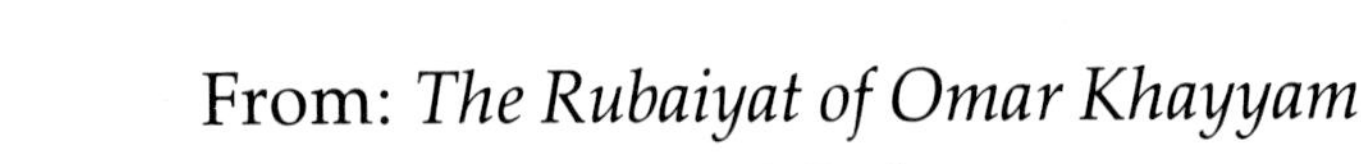

From: *The Rubaiyat of Omar Khayyam*

COME, fill the cup, and in the fire of spring
Your winter-garment of repentance fling;
  The bird of time has but a little way
To flutter — and the bird is on the wing.

Whether at Naishápur or Babylon,
Whether the cup with sweet or bitter run,
  The wine of life keeps oozing drop by drop,
The leaves of life keep falling one by one.

Each morn a thousand roses brings, you say;
Yes, but where leaves the rose of yesterday?
  And this first summer month that brings the rose
Shall take Jamshyd and Kaikobád away.

Well, let it take them! What have we to do
With Kaikobád the Great, or Kaikhosrú?
  Let Zál and Rustum bluster as they will,
Or Hátim call to supper — heed not you.

With me along the strip of herbage strown
That just divides the desert from the sown,
  Where name of slave and sultán is forgot —
And peace to Mahmúd on his golden throne!

A book of verses underneath the bough,
A jug of wine, a loaf of bread — and thou
  Beside me singing in the wilderness —
Oh, wilderness were paradise enow!

EDWARD FITZGERALD (1809–1883)

Invictus

OUT of the night that covers me,
  Black as the pit from pole to pole,
I thank whatever gods may be
  For my unconquerable soul.

In the fell clutch of circumstance
  I have not winced nor cried aloud;
Under the bludgeonings of chance
  My head is bloody, but unbow'd.

Beyond this place of wrath and tears
  Looms but the Horror of the Shade,
And yet the menace of the years
  Finds and shall find me unafraid.

It matters not how strait the gate,
  How charged with punishments the scroll,
I am the master of my fate:
  I am the captain of my soul.

WILLIAM HENLEY (1849–1903)

The Listeners

'IS THERE anybody there?' said the Traveller,
  Knocking on the mooonlit door;
And his horse in the silence champ'd the grasses
  Of the forest's ferny floor:
And a bird flew up out of the turret,
  Above the Traveller's head:
And he smote upon the door again a second time;
  'Is there anybody there?' he said.
But no one descended to the Traveller;
  No head from the leaf-fringed sill
Lean'd over and look'd into his grey eyes,
  Where he stood perplex'd and still.
But only a host of phantom listeners
  That dwelt in the lone house then
Stood listening in the quiet of the moonlight
  To that voice from the world of men:
Stood thronging the faint moonbeams on the dark stair,
  That goes down to the empty hall,
Hearkening in an air stirr'd and shaken
  By the lonely Traveller's call.
And he felt in his heart their strangeness,
  Their stillness answering his cry,
While his horse moved, cropping the dark turf,
  'Neath the starr'd and leafy sky;
For he suddenly smote on the door, even
  Louder, and lifted his head: —
'Tell them I came, and no one answer'd,
  That I kept my word,' he said.
Never the least stir made the listeners,
  Though every word he spake
Fell echoing through the shadowiness of the still house
  From the one man left awake:
Ay, they heard his foot upon the stirrup,
  And the sound of iron on stone,
And how the silence surged softly backward,
  When the plunging hoofs were gone.

WALTER DE LA MARE (1873–1956)

On His Blindness

When I consider how my light is spent
Ere half my days, in this dark world and wide,
And that one talent which is death to hide
Lodged with me useless, though my soul more bent

To serve therewith my Maker, and present
My true account, lest He returning chide, —
Doth God exact day-labour, light denied?
I fondly ask: — But Patience, to prevent

That murmur, soon replies; God doth not need
Either man's work, or His own gifts: who best
Bear His mild yoke, they serve Him best: His state

Is kingly; thousands at His bidding speed
And post o'er land and ocean without rest: —
They also serve who only stand and wait.

John Milton (1608–1674)

The Blessèd Damozel

The blessèd damozel lean'd out
  From the gold bar of Heaven;
Her eyes were deeper than the depth
  Of waters stilled at even;
She had three lilies in her hand,
  And the stars in her hair were seven.

Her robe, ungirt from clasp to hem,
  No wrought flowers did adorn,
But a white rose of Mary's gift
  On the neck meetly worn;
And her hair, lying down her back,
  Was yellow like ripe corn.

Herseemed she scarce had been a day
  One of God's choristers;
The wonder was not yet quite gone
  From that still look of hers;
Albeit, to them she left, her day
  Had counted as ten years.

(To one, it is ten years of years.
  . . . Yet now, and in this place,
Surely she leaned o'er me, — her hair
  Fell about about my face . . .
Nothing: the Autumn-fall of leaves.
  The whole year sets apace.)

It was the rampart of God's house
  That she was standing on, —
By God built over the sheer depth
  In which is Space begun;
So high, that looking downward thence
  She scarce could see the sun.

It lies in Heaven, across the flood
  Of ether, as a bridge.
Beneath, the tides of day and night
  With flame and darkness ridge
The void, as low as where this earth
  Spins like a fretful midge.

Heard hardly, some of her new friends
  Amid their loving games,
Spake evermore, among themselves,
  Their virginal chaste names;
And the souls, mounting up to God
  Went by her like thin flames.

And still she bowed herself and stooped
  Out of the circling charm;
Until her bosom must have made
  The bar she leaned on warm,
And the lilies lay as if asleep
  Along her bended arm.

From the fixed place of Heaven she saw
  Time like a pulse shake fierce
Through all the worlds. Her gaze still strove
  In that steep gulf, to pierce
Its path; and then she spoke as when
  The stars sang in their spheres.

The sun was gone now; the curled moon
  Was like a little feather
Fluttering far down the gulf; and now
  She spoke through the still weather.
Her voice was like the voice the stars
  Had when they sang together.

(Ah sweet! Even now, in that bird's song,
  Strove not her accents there,
Fain to be hearkened? When those bells
  Possessed the mid-day air,
Strove not her steps to reach my side
  Down all the echoing stair?)

'I wish that he were come to me,
  For he will come,' she said.
'Have I not prayed in Heaven?—on earth,
  Lord, Lord, has he not prayed?
Are not two prayers a perfect strength?
  And shall I feel afraid?

'When round his head the aureole clings,
  And he is clothed in white,
I'll take his hand, and go with him
  To the deep wells of light;
And we will step down as to a stream,
  And bathe there in God's sight.

'We two will stand beside that shrine,
  Occult, withheld, untrod,
Whose lamps are stirred continually
  With prayer sent up to God;
And see our old prayers, granted, melt
  Each like a little cloud.

'We two will lie i' the shadow of
  That living mystic tree
Within whose secret growth the Dove
  Sometimes is felt to be,
While every leaf that His plumes touch
  Saith His name audibly.

'And I myself will teach to him,
  I myself, lying so,
The songs I sing here; which his voice
  Shall pause in, hushed and slow,
Finding some knowledge at each pause,
  And some new thing to know.'

(Alas! We two, we two, thou say'st!
  Yea, one wast thou with me
That once of old. But shall God lift
  To endless unity
The soul whose likeness with thy soul
  Was but its love for thee?)

'We two,' she said, 'will seek the groves
  Where the lady Mary is,
With her five handmaidens, whose names
  Are five sweet symphonies,—
Cecily, Gertrude, Magdalen,
  Margaret and Rosalys.

'Circlewise sit they, with bound locks
  And foreheads garlanded;
Into the fine cloth, white like flame,
  Weaving the golden thread,
To fashion the birth-robes for them
  Who are just born, being dead.

'He shall fear, haply, and be dumb:
  Then I will lay my cheek
To his, and tell about our love,
  Not once abash'd or weak:
And the dear Mother will approve
  My pride, and let me speak.

Dante Gabriel Rossetti (1828–1882) *The Blessed Damozel* (detail), Fogg Museum of Art, Harvard

Claude Monet (1840–1926) *Waterlilies*, Private Collection

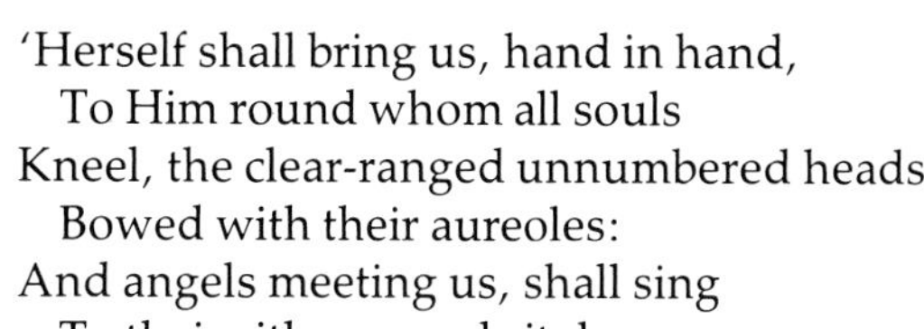

'Herself shall bring us, hand in hand,
To Him round whom all souls
Kneel, the clear-ranged unnumbered heads
Bowed with their aureoles:
And angels meeting us, shall sing
To their citherns and citoles.

'There will I ask of Christ the Lord
Thus much for him and me: —
To have more blessing than on earth
With Love, — only to be
As then awhile, for ever now
Together, I and he:'

She gazed, and listened, and then said,
Less sad of speech than mild, —
'All this is when he comes.' She ceased.
The light thrilled towards her, filled
With angels, in strong level flight.
Her eyes prayed, and she smiled.

(I saw her smile.) But soon their path
Was vague in distant spheres.
And then she cast her arms along
The golden barriers,
And laid her face between her hands,
And wept. (I heard her tears.)

DANTE GABRIEL ROSSETTI (1828–1882)

From: *Ballad of Reading Gaol*

In Reading gaol by Reading town
  There is a pit of shame,
And in it lies a wretched man
  Eaten by teeth of flame,
In a burning winding-sheet he lies,
  And his grave has got no name.

And there, till Christ call forth the dead,
  In silence let him lie:
No need to waste the foolish tear,
  Or heave the windy sigh:
The man had killed the thing he loved,
  And so he had to die.

And all men kill the thing they love,
  By all let this be heard,
Some do it with a bitter look,
  Some with a flattering word,
The coward does it with a kiss,
  The brave man with a sword!

Oscar Wilde (1854–1900)

JOURNEYINGS

Night Mail
(Commentary for a G.P.O. Film)

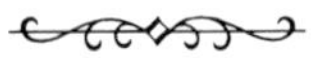

I

THIS is the Night Mail crossing the Border,
Bringing the cheque and the postal order,

Letters for the rich, letters for the poor,
The shop at the corner, the girl next door.

Pulling up Beattock, a steady climb:
The gradient's against her, but she's on time.

Past cotton-grass and moorland boulder,
Shovelling white steam over her shoulder,

Snorting noisily, she passes
Silent miles of wind-bent grasses.

Birds turn their heads as she approaches,
Stare from bushes at her blank-faced coaches.

Sheep-dogs cannot turn her course;
They slumber on with paws across.

In the farm she passes no one wakes,
But a jug in a bedroom gently shakes.

II

Dawn freshens. Her climb is done.
Down towards Glasgow she descends,
Towards the steam tugs yelping down a glade of cranes,
Towards the fields of apparatus, the furnaces
Set on the dark plain like gigantic chessmen.
All Scotland waits for her:
In dark glens, beside pale-green lochs,
Men long for news.

III

Letters of thanks, letters from banks,
Letters of joy from girl and boy,
Receipted bills and invitations
To inspect new stock or to visit relations,
And applications for situations,
And timid lovers' declarations,
And gossip, gossip from all the nations,
News circumstantial, news financial,
Letters with holiday snaps to enlarge in,
Letters from uncles, cousins and aunts,
Letters to Scotland from the South of France,
Letters of condolence to Highlands and Lowlands,
Written on paper of every hue,
The pink, the violet, the white and the blue,
The chatty, the catty, the boring, the adoring,
The cold and official and the heart's outpouring,
Clever, stupid, short and long,
The typed and the printed and the spelt all wrong.

IV

Thousands are still asleep,
Dreaming of terrifying monsters
Or a friendly tea beside the band in Cranston's or Crawford's:
Asleep in working Glasgow, asleep in well-set Edinburgh,
Asleep in granite Aberdeen,
They continue their dreams,
But shall wake soon and hope for letters,
And none will hear the postman's knock
Without a quickening of the heart
For who can bear to feel himself forgotten?

W. H. AUDEN (1907–1973)

The Journey of The Magi

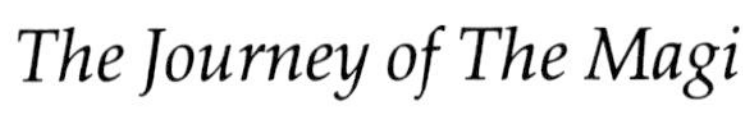

'A COLD coming we had of it,
Just the worst time of the year
For a journey, and such a long journey:
The ways deep and the weather sharp,
The very dead of winter.'
And the camels galled, sore-footed, refractory,
Lying down in the melting snow.
There were times we regretted
The summer palaces on slopes, the terraces,
And the silken girls bringing sherbet.
Then the camel men cursing and grumbling
And running away, and wanting their liquor and women,
And the night-fires going out, and the lack of shelters,
And the cities hostile and the towns unfriendly
And the villages dirty and charging high prices:
A hard time we had of it.
At the end we preferred to travel all night,
Sleeping in snatches,
With the voices singing in our ears, saying
That this was all folly.

Then at dawn we came down to a temperate valley,
Wet, below the snow line, smelling of vegetation;
With a running stream and a water-mill beating the darkness,
And three trees on the low sky.
And an old white horse galloped away in the meadow.
Then we came to a tavern with vine-leaves over the lintel,
Six hands at an open foor dicing for pieces of silver,
And feet kicking the empty wine-skins.
But there was no information, and so we continued
And arrived at evening, not a moment too soon
Finding the place; it was (you may say) satisfactory.

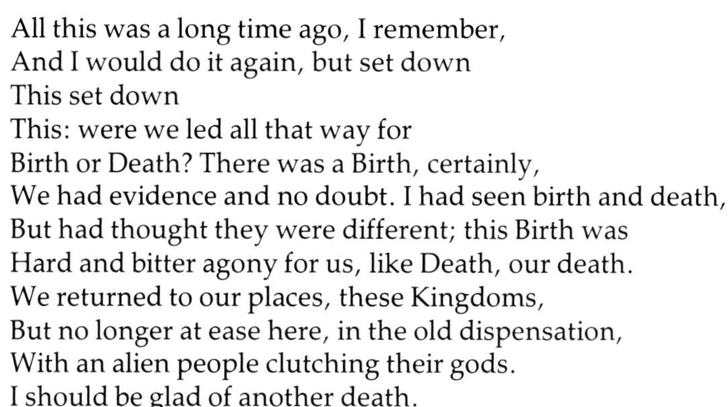

All this was a long time ago, I remember,
And I would do it again, but set down
This set down
This: were we led all that way for
Birth or Death? There was a Birth, certainly,
We had evidence and no doubt. I had seen birth and death,
But had thought they were different; this Birth was
Hard and bitter agony for us, like Death, our death.
We returned to our places, these Kingdoms,
But no longer at ease here, in the old dispensation,
With an alien people clutching their gods.
I should be glad of another death.

T. S. ELIOT (1888–1965)

Uphill

DOES the road wind uphill all the way?
  Yes, to the very end.
Will the day's journey take the whole long day?
  From morn to night, my friend.

But is there for the night a resting-place?
  A roof for when the slow, dark hours begin.
May not the darkness hide it from my face?
  You cannot miss that inn.

Shall I meet other wayfarers at night?
  Those who have gone before.
Then must I knock, or call when just in sight?
  They will not keep you waiting at that door.

Shall I find comfort, travel-sore and weak?
  Of labour you shall find the sum.
Will there be beds for me and all who seek?
  Yea, beds for all who come.

CHRISTINA ROSSETTI (1830–1894)

The Vagabond

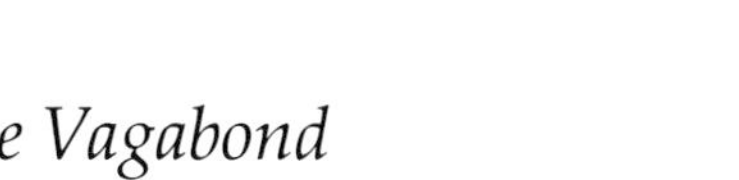

GIVE to me the life I love,
  Let the lave go by me,
Give the jolly heaven above
  And the by-way nigh me.
Bed in the bush with stars to see,
  Bread I dip in the river —
There's the life for a man like me,
  There's the life for ever.

Let the blow fall soon or late,
  Let what will be o'er me:
Give the face of earth around
  And the road before me.
Wealth I seek not, hope nor love,
  Nor a friend to know me;
All I seek, the heaven above
  And the road below me.

Or let autumn fall on me
  Where afield I linger,
Silencing the bird on tree
  Biting the blue finger.
White as meal the frosty field —
  Warm the fireside haven —
Not to autumn will I yield,
  Not to winter even!

Let the blow fall soon or late,
  Let what will be o'er me;
Give the face of earth around,
  And the road before me.
Wealth I ask not, hope nor love,
  Nor a friend to know me;
All I ask, the heaven above,
  And the road below me.

ROBERT LOUIS STEVENSON (1850–1894)

Ulysses

IT LITTLE profits that an idle king,
By this still hearth, among these barren crags,
Matched with an agèd wife, I mete and dole
Unequal laws unto a savage race,
That hoard, and sleep, and feed, and know not me.
I cannot rest from travel: I will drink
Life to the lees: all times I have enjoyed
Greatly, have suffered greatly, both with those
That loved me, and alone; on shore, and when
Thro' scudding drifts the rainy Hyades
Vext the dim sea: I am become a name;
For always roaming with a hungry heart
Much have I seen and known; cities of men
And manners, climates, councils, governments,
Myself not least, but honoured of them all;
And drunk delight of battle with my peers,
Far on the ringing plains of windy Troy.
I am a part of all that I have met;
Yet all experience is an arch wherethro'
Gleams that untravelled world, whose margin fades
For ever and for ever when I move.
How dull it is to pause, to make an end,
To rust unburnished, not to shine in use!
As tho' to breathe were life. Life piled on life
Were all too little, and of one to me
Little remains: but every hour is saved
From that eternal silence, something more,
A bringer of new things; and vile it were
For some three suns to store and hoard myself,
And this grey spirit yearning in desire
To follow knowledge like a sinking star,
Beyond the utmost bound of human thought.

This is my son, mine own Telemachus,
To whom I leave the sceptre and the isle —
Well-loved of me, discerning to fulfil
This labour, by slow prudence to make mild
A rugged people, and thro' soft degrees
Subdue them to the useful and the good.
Most blameless is he, centred in the sphere
Of common duties, decent not to fail
In offices of tenderness, and pay
Meet adoration to my household gods,
When I am gone. He works his work, I mine.
There lies the port: the vessel puffs her sail:
There gloom the dark broad seas. My mariners,
Souls that have toiled, and wrought, and thought with me —
That ever with a frolic welcome took
The thunder and the sunshine, and opposed
Free hearts, free foreheads — you and I are old;
Old age hath yet his honour and his toil;
Death closes all: but something ere the end,
Some work of noble note, may yet be done,
Not unbecoming men that strove with Gods.
The lights begin to twinkle from the rocks:
The long day wanes: the slow moon climbs: the deep
Moans round with many voices. Come, my friends,
'Tis not too late to seek a newer world.
Push off, and sitting well in order smite
The sounding furrows; for my purpose holds
To sail beyond the sunset, and the baths
Of all the western stars, until I die.
It may be that the gulfs will wash us down:
It may be we shall touch the Happy Isles,
And see the great Achilles, whom we knew.
Tho' much is taken, much abides; and tho'
We are not now that strength which in old days
Moved earth and heaven; that which we are, we are;
One equal temper of heroic hearts,
Made weak by time and fate, but strong in will
To strive, to seek, to find, and not to yield.

ALFRED LORD TENNYSON (1809–1892)

Adlestrop

YES. I remember Adlestrop —
The name, because one afternoon
Of heat the express-train drew up there
Unwontedly. It was late June.

The steam hissed. Someone cleared his throat
No one left and no one came
On the bare platform. What I saw
Was Adlestrop — only the name

And willows, willow-herb, and grass,
And meadowsweet, and haycocks dry,
No whit less still and lonely fair
Than the high cloudlets in the sky.

And for that minute a blackbird sang
Close by, and round him, mistier,
Farther and farther, all the birds
Of Oxfordshire and Gloucestershire.

EDWARD THOMAS (1878–1917)

O Captain! my Captain!

O CAPTAIN! my Captain! our fearful trip is done!
The ship has wreathed every wrack,
the prize we sought is won.
The port is near, the bells I hear,
the people all exulting,
While follow eyes the steady keel,
the vessel grim and daring.
But, O heart! heart! heart!
Leave you not the little spot
Where on the deck my Captain lies,
Fallen cold and dead.

O Captain! my Captain! rise up and hear the bells;
Rise up — for you the flag is flung —
for you the bugle trills,
For you bouquets and ribbon'd wreaths —
for you the shores a-crowding,
For you they call, the swaying mass,
their eager faces turning.
Here, Captain, dear father!
This arm I push beneath you.
It is some dream that on the deck
You've fallen cold and dead.

My Captain does not answer, his lips are pale and still,
My father does not feel my arm,
he has no pulse nor will;
The ship is anchor'd safe and sound,
its voyage closed and done,
From fearful trip the victor ship
comes in with object won;
Exult, O shores! and ring, O bells!
But I, with silent tread,
Walk the spot my Captain lies,
Fallen cold and dead.

WALT WHITMAN (1819–1892)

NATURE

Tiger!

TIGER! Tiger burning bright
In the forests of the night,
What immortal hand or eye
Could frame thy fearful symmetry?

In what distant deeps or skies
Burnt the fire of thine eyes?
On what wings dare he aspire?
What the hand dare seize the fire?

And what shoulder, and what art,
Could twist the sinews of thy heart?
And, when thy heart began to beat,
What dread hand? and what dread feet?

What the hammer? what the chain?
In what furnace was thy brain?
What the anvil? what dread grasp
Dare its deadly terrors clasp?

When the stars threw down their spears,
And watered heaven with their tears,
Did he smile His work to see?
Did he who made the Lamb make thee?

Tiger! Tiger! burning bright
In the forests of the night,
What immortal hand or eye
Dare frame thy fearful symmetry?

WILLIAM BLAKE (1757–1827)

The Sick Rose

O ROSE, thou art sick!
The invisible worm
That flies in the night,
In the howling storm,

Has found out thy bed
Of crimson joy,
And his dark secret love
Does thy life destroy.

WILLIAM BLAKE (1757–1827)

The Old Squire

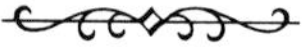

I LIKE the hunting of the hare
  Better than that of the fox;
I like the joyous morning air,
  And the crowing of the cocks.

I like the calm of the early fields,
  The ducks asleep by the lake,
The quiet hour which Nature yields,
  Before mankind is awake.

I like the pheasants and feeding things
  Of the unsuspicious morn;
I like the flap of the wood-pigeon's wings
  As she rises from the corn.

I like the blackbird's shriek, and his rush
  From the turnips as I pass by,
And the partridge hiding her head in a bush,
  For her young ones cannot fly.

Henri Rousseau (1844–1910) *Tropical Storm with a Tiger* (detail), National Gallery, London

Samuel Palmer (1805–1881) *A Shoreham Garden,* Victoria and Albert Museum, London

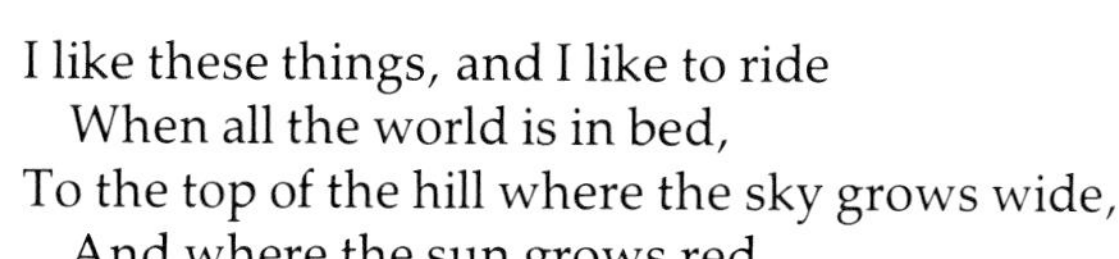

I like these things, and I like to ride
When all the world is in bed,
To the top of the hill where the sky grows wide,
And where the sun grows red.

The beagles at my horse heels trot
In silence after me;
There's Ruby, Roger, Diamond, Dot,
Old Slut and Margery, —

A score of names well used, and dear,
The names my childhood knew;
The horn, with which I rouse their cheer,
Is the horn my father blew.

I like the hunting of the hare
Better than that of the fox;
The new world still is all less fair
Than the old world it mocks.

I covet not a wider range
Than these dear manors give;
I take my pleasure without change,
And as I lived I live.

I leave my neighbours to their thought;
My choice it is, and pride
On my own lands to find my sport,
In my own fields to ride.

The hare herself no better loves
The field where she was bred,
Than I the habit of these groves,
My own inherited.

I know my quarries every one,
The meuse where she sits low;
The road she chose to-day was run
A hundred years ago.

The lags, the gills, the forest ways,
  The hedgerows one and all,
These are the kingdoms of my chase,
  And bounded by my wall;

Nor has the world a better thing,
  Though one should search it round,
Than thus to live one's own sole king,
  Upon one's own sole ground.

I like the hunting of the hare;
  It brings me, day by day,
The memory of old days as fair,
  With dead men past away.

To these, as homeward still I ply,
  And pass the churchyard gate
Where all are laid as I must lie,
  I stop and raise my hat.

I like the hunting of the hare;
  New sports I hold in scorn.
I like to be as my fathers were,
  In the days ere I was born.

WILFRID SCAWEN BLUNT (1840–1922)

London Snow

WHEN men were all asleep the snow came flying,
In large white flakes falling on the city brown,
Stealthily and perpetually settling and loosely lying,
  Hushing the latest traffic of the drowsy town;
Deadening, muffling, stifling its murmurs failing;
Lazily and incessantly floating down and down:
  Silently sifting and veiling road, roof and railing;
Hiding difference, making unevenness even,
Into angles and crevices softly drifting and sailing.
  All night it fell, and when full inches seven
It lay in the depth of its uncompacted lightness,
The clouds blew off from a high and frosty heaven;
  And all woke earlier for the unaccustomed brightness
Of the winter dawning, the strange unheavenly glare:
The eye marvelled — marvelled at the dazzling whiteness;
  The ear hearkened to the stillness of the solemn air;
No sound of wheel rumbling nor of foot falling,
And the busy morning cries came thin and spare.
  Then boys I heard, as they went to school, calling,
They gathered up the crystal manna to freeze
Their tongues with tasting, their hands with snowballing;
  Or rioted in a drift, plunging up to the knees;
Or peering up from under the white-mossed wonder,
'O look at the trees!' they cried, 'O look at the trees!'
  With lessened load a few carts creak and blunder,
Following along the white deserted way,
A country company long dispersed asunder:
  When now already the sun, in pale display
Standing by Paul's high dome, spread forth below
His sparkling beams, and awoke the stir of the day.

  For now doors open, and war is waged with the snow;
And trains of sombre men, past tale of number,
Tread long brown paths, as toward their toil they go:
  But even for them awhile no cares encumber
Their minds diverted; the daily word is unspoken,
The daily thoughts of labour and sorrow slumber
At the sight of the beauty that greets them, for the charm they have broken.

ROBERT BRIDGES (1844–1930)

To a Field Mouse

Wee, sleekit, cow'rin', tim'rous beastie,
O what a panic's in thy breastie!
Thou need na start awa sae hasty,
Wi' bickering brattle!
I wad be laith to rin an' chase thee
Wi' murd'ring pattle!

I'm truly sorry man's dominion
Has broken nature's social union,
An' justifies that ill opinion
Which makes thee startle
At me, thy poor earth-born companion,
An' fellow-mortal!

I doubt na, whiles, but thou may thieve;
What then? poor beastie, thou maun live!
A daimen-icker in a thrave
'S a sma' request:
I'll get a blessin' wi' the lave,
And never miss't!

Thy wee bit housie, too, in ruin!
Its silly wa's the win's are strewin':
And naething, now, to big a new ane,
O' foggage green!
An' bleak December's winds ensuin'
Baith snell an' keen!

Thou saw the fields laid bare and waste
An' weary winter comin' fast,
An' cozie here, beneath the blast,
Thou thought to dwell,
Till, crash! the cruel coulter past
Out thro' thy cell.

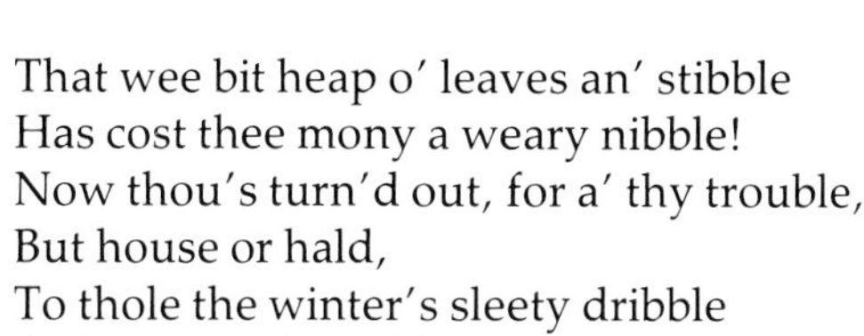

That wee bit heap o' leaves an' stibble
Has cost thee mony a weary nibble!
Now thou's turn'd out, for a' thy trouble,
But house or hald,
To thole the winter's sleety dribble
An' cranreuch cauld!

But, Mousie, thou art no thy lane
In proving foresight may be vain:
The best laid schemes o' mice an' men
Gang aft a-gley,
An' lea'e us nought but grief an' pain,
For promised joy.

Still thou art blest, compared wi' me!
The present only toucheth thee:
But, oh! I backward cast my e'e
On prospects drear!
An' forward, tho' I canna see,
I guess an' fear!

Robert Burns (1759–1796)

The Donkey

WHEN fishes flew and forests walked
And figs grew upon thorn,
Some moment when the moon was blood
Then surely I was born;

With monstrous head and sickening cry
And ears like errant wings,
The devil's walking parody
On all four-footed things.

The tattered outlaw of the earth,
Of ancient crooked will;
Starve, scourge, deride me: I am dumb,
I keep my secret still.

Fools! For I also had my hour;
One far fierce hour and sweet:
There was a shout about my ears,
And palms before my feet.

G. K. CHESTERTON (1874–1936)

A Narrow Fellow in the Grass

A NARROW fellow in the grass
Occasionally rides;
You may have met him, — did you not?
His notice sudden is.

The grass divides as with a comb,
A spotted shaft is seen;
And then it closes at your feet
And opens further on.

He likes a boggy acre,
A floor too cool for corn.
Yet when a child, and barefoot,
I more than once, at morn,

Have passed, I thought, a whip-lash
Upbraiding in the sun, —
When, stooping to secure it,
It wrinkled, and was gone.

Several of nature's people
I know, and they know me;
I feel for them a transport
Of cordiality;

But never met this fellow,
Attended or alone,
Without a tighter breathing,
And zero at the bone.

EMILY DICKINSON (1830–1886)

Elegy on the Death of a Mad Dog

Good people all, of every sort,
  Give ear unto my song;
And if you find it wond'rous short,
  It cannot hold you long.

In Islington there was a man,
  Of whom the world might say,
That still a godly race he ran,
  Whene'er he went to pray.

A kind and gentle heart he had,
  To comfort friends and foes;
The naked every day he clad,
  When he put on his clothes.

And in that town a dog was found,
  As many dogs there be,
Both mongrel, puppy, whelp, and hound,
  And curs of low degree.

This dog and man at first were friends;
  But when a pique began,
The dog, to gain some private ends,
  Went mad and bit the man.

Around from all the neighbouring streets
  The wond'ring neighbours ran,
And swore the dog had lost his wits,
  To bite so good a man.

The wound it seemed both sore and sad
  To every Christian eye;
And while they swore the dog was mad,
  They swore the man would die.

But soon a wonder came to light,
  That showed the rogues they lied:
The man recovered of the bite,
  The dog it was that died.

Oliver Goldsmith (1730–1774)

The Darkling Thrush

I LEANT upon a coppice gate
  When Frost was spectre-grey,
And Winter's dregs made desolate
  The weakening eye of day.
The tangled bine-stems scored the sky
  Like strings of broken lyres,
And all mankind that haunted nigh
  Had sought their household fires.

The land's sharp features seemed to be
  The Century's corpse outleant,
His crypt the cloudy canopy,
  The wind his death-lament.
The ancient pulse of germ and birth
  Was shrunken hard and dry,
And every spirit upon earth
  Seemed fervourless as I.

At once a voice arose among
  The bleak twigs overhead
In a full-hearted evensong
  Of joy illimited;
An aged thrush, frail, gaunt, and small,
  In blast-beruffled plume,
Had chosen thus to fling his soul
  Upon the growing gloom.

So little cause for carollings
  Of such ecstatic sound
Was written on terrestrial things
  Afar or nigh around,
That I could think there trembled through
  His happy good-night air
Some blessed Hope, whereof he knew
  And I was unaware.

THOMAS HARDY (1840–1928)

To Autumn

SEASON of mists and mellow fruitfulness,
  Close bosom-friend of the maturing sun;
Conspiring with him how to load and bless
  With fruit the vines that round the thatch-eves run;
To bend with apples the moss'd cottage-trees,
  And fill all fruit with ripeness to the core;
    To swell the gourd, and plump the hazel shells
  With a sweet kernel; to set budding more,
And still more, later flowers for the bees,
Until they think warm days will never cease,
  For Summer has o'er-brimm'd their clammy cells.

Who hath not seen thee oft amid thy store?
  Sometimes whoever seeks abroad may find
Thee sitting careless on a granary floor,
  Thy hair soft-lifted by the winnowing wind;
Or on a half-reap'd furrow sound asleep,
  Drows'd with the fume of poppies, while thy hook
    Spares the next swath and all its twined flowers:
And sometimes like a gleaner thou dost keep
  Steady thy laden head across a brook;
  Or by a cyder-press, with patient look,
    Thou watchest the last oozings hours by hours.

Where are the songs of Spring? Ay, where are they?
  Think not of them, thou hast thy music too, —
While barred clouds bloom the soft-dying day,
  And touch the stubble-plains with rosy hue;
Then in a wailful choir the small gnats mourn
  Among the river sallows, borne aloft
    Or sinking as the light wind lives or dies;
And full-grown lambs loud bleat from hilly bourn;
  Hedge-crickets sing; and now with treble soft
  The red-breast whistles from a garden-croft;
    And gathering swallows twitter in the skies.

JOHN KEATS (1795–1821)

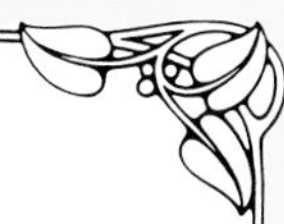

Sea-Fever

I MUST go down to the seas again, to the lonely sea and the sky,
And all I ask is a tall ship and a star to steer her by,
And the wheel's kick and the wind's song and the white sails shaking,
And a grey mist on the sea's face and a grey dawn breaking.

I must go down to the seas again, for the call of the running tide
Is a wild call and a clear call that may not be denied;
And all I ask is a windy day with the white clouds flying,
And the flung spray and the blown spume, and the sea-gulls crying.

I must go down to the seas again, to the vagrant gypsy life,
To the gull's way and the whale's way where the wind's like a whetted knife;
And all I ask is a merry yarn from a laughing fellow-rover,
And quiet sleep and a sweet dream when the long trick's over.

JOHN MASEFIELD (1878–1967)

WAR

Into Battle

THE naked earth is warm with Spring,
  And with green grass and bursting trees
Leans to the sun's gaze glorying,
  And quivers in the sunny breeze;
And life is Colour and Warmth and Light,
  And a striving evermore for these;
And he is dead who will not fight,
  And who dies fighting has increase.

The fighting man shall from the sun
  Take warmth, and life from the glowing earth;
Speed with the light-foot winds to run,
  And with the trees to newer birth;
And find, when fighting shall be done,
  Great rest, and fullness after dearth.

All the bright company of Heaven
  Hold him in their high comradeship,
The Dog-star, and the Sisters Seven,
Orion's Belt and sworded hip.

The woodland trees that stand together,
  They stand to him each one a friend;
They gently speak in the windy weather;
  They guide to valley and ridge's end.

The kestrel hovering by day,
  And the little owls that call by night,
Bid him be swift and keen as they,
  As keen of ear, as swift of sight.

The blackbird sings to him, 'Brother, brother,
  If this be the last song you shall sing
Sing well, for you may not sing another;
  Brother, sing.'

In dreary doubtful waiting hours,
  Before the brazen frenzy starts,
The horses show him nobler powers; —
  O patient eyes, courageous hearts!

And when the burning moment breaks,
  And all things else are out of mind,
And only Joy of Battle takes
  Him by the throat and makes him blind,

Through joy and blindness he shall know,
  Not caring much to know, that still
Nor lead nor steel shall reach him, so
  That it be not the Destined Will.

The thundering line of battle stands,
  And in the air Death moans and sings;
But Day shall clasp him with strong hands,
  And Night shall fold him in soft wings.

JULIAN GRENFELL (1888–1915)

To Lucasta, on Going to the Wars

TELL me not, Sweet, I am unkind
  That from the nunnery
Of thy chaste breast and quiet mind,
  To war and arms I fly.

True, a new mistress now I chase,
  The first foe in the field;
And with a stronger faith embrace
  A sword, a horse, a shield.

Yet this inconstancy is such
  As you too shall adore;
I could not love thee, Dear, so much,
  Loved I not Honour more.

RICHARD LOVELACE (1616–1658)

Returned Soldier

I Put him on the train in Albury
The night he went to take his boat, and he,
Swinging aboard, called gaily, 'Don't forget,
I'll dodge them all and be a farmer yet.
And raise, for every bullet that goes by,
A stalk of wheat, red-gold and shoulder high,
Three hundred acres, lad!' And then the train
Was gone. The night was loud with frogs again.

And five years later, one November day,
I walked with Barry down the stooks of hay
Light yellow in the sun, and on them fluttered
Rosellas red as apples. Barry muttered
Half shyly as we faced the level wheat:
'One good foot left of what was once two feet,
One lung just fair, and one unclouded eye;
But all those years I heard them whining by
And in the mud I chuckled to remember
How wheat turns copper and gold in late November.'
He smiled, and then I knew what charm had brought
Him safely past the 'world's great snare', uncaught.

E. G. Moll (1900–)

The Death of Admiral Blake

(August 7th, 1657)

LADEN with spoil of the South, fulfilled with the glory of
achievement,
And freshly crowned with never-dying fame,
Sweeping by shores where the names are the names of
the victories of England
Across the Bay the squadron homeward came.

Proudly they came, but their pride was the pomp of a
funeral at midnight,
When the dreader yet the lonely morrow looms;
Few are the words that are spoken, and faces are gaunt
beneath the torchlight
That does but darken more the nodding plumes.

Low on the field of his fame, past hope lay the Admiral
triumphant,
And fain to rest him after all his pain;
Yet for the love that he bore to his own land, ever
unforgotten,
He prayed to see the western hills again.

Fainter than stars in a sky long grey with the coming of
the daybreak,
Or sounds of night that fade when night is done,
So in the death-dawn faded the splendour and loud
renown of warfare,
And life of all its longings kept but one.

'Oh! to be there for an hour when the shade draws in
beside the hedgerows,
And falling apples wake the drowsy noon:
Oh! for the hour when the elms grow sombre and
human in the twilight,
And gardens dream beneath the rising moon.

'Only to look once more on the land of the memories of
childhood,
Forgetting weary winds and barren foam:
Only to bid farewell to the combe and the orchard and
the moorland,
And sleep at last among the fields of home!'

J. M. W. Turner (1775–1851) *Peace: Burial at Sea,* Tate Gallery, London

Edvard Munch (1863–1944) *The Scream,* Nasjonalgalleriet, Oslo

So he was silently praying, till now, when his strength
was ebbing faster,
The Lizard lay before them faintly blue;
Now on the gleaming horizon the white cliffs laughed
along the coast-line,
And now the forelands took the shapes they knew.

There lay the Sound and the Island with green leaves
down beside the water,
The town, the Hoe, the masts with sunset fired —
Dreams! ay, dreams of the dead! for the great heart
faltered on the threshold,
And darkness took the land his soul desired.

HENRY NEWBOLT (1862–1938)

Anthem for Doomed Youth

WHAT passing-bells for these who die as cattle?
Only the monstrous anger of the guns.
Only the stuttering rifles' rapid rattle
Can patter out their hasty orisons.
No mockeries now for them; no prayers nor bells,
Nor any voice of mourning save the choirs,—
The shrill, demented choirs of wailing shells;
And bugles calling for them from sad shires.

What candles may be held to speed them all?
Not in the hands of boys, but in their eyes
Shall shine the holy glimmers of good-byes.
The pallor of girls' brows shall be their pall;
Their flowers the tenderness of patient minds,
And each slow dusk a drawing-down of blinds.

WILFRED OWEN (1893–1918)

For Johnny

Do not despair
For Johnny-head-in-air;
He sleeps as sound
As Johnny underground.

Fetch out no shroud
For Johnny-in-the-cloud;
And keep your tears
For him in after years.

Better by far
For Johnny-the-bright-star,
To keep your head,
And see his children fed.

JOHN PUDNEY (1909–1977)

On Receiving News of the War

SNOW is a strange white word.
No ice or frost
Has asked of bud or bird
For Winter's cost.

Yet ice and frost and snow
From earth to sky
This Summer land doth know.
No man knows why.

In all men's hearts it is.
Some spirit old
Hath turned with malign kiss
Our lives to mould.

Red fangs have torn His face.
God's blood is shed.
He mourns from His lone place
His children dead.

O! ancient crimson curse!
Corrode, consume.
Give back this universe
Its pristine bloom.

ISAAC ROSENBERG (1890-1918)

Aftermath

Have you forgotten yet? . . .
For the world's events have rumbled on since those
gagged days,
Like traffic checked awhile at the crossing of city ways:
And the haunted gap in your mind has filled with thoughts
that flow
Like clouds in the lit heaven of life; and you're a man
reprieved to go,
Taking your peaceful share of Time, with joy to spare.
But the past is just the same, — and War's a bloody game . . .
Have you forgotten yet? . . .
*Look down and swear by the slain of the War that you'll never
forget.*

Do you remember the dark months you held the sector at
Mametz, —
The nights you watched and wired and dug and piled
sandbags on parapets?
Do you remember the rats; and the stench
Of corpses rotting in front of the front-line trench, —
And dawn coming, dirty-white, and chill with a hopeless
rain?
Do you ever stop and ask, 'Is it all going to happen again?'

Do you remember that hour of din before the attack, —
And the anger, the blind compassion that seized and
shook you then
As you peered at the doomed and haggard faces of your
men?
Do you remember the stretcher-cases lurching back
With dying eyes and lolling heads, — those ashen-grey
Masks of the lads who once were keen and kind and
gay?
Have you forgotten yet? . . .
*Look up, and swear by the green of the Spring that you'll never
forget.*

SIEGFRIED SASSOON (1886–1967)

Rendezvous

I HAVE a rendezvous with Death
At some disputed barricade,
When Spring comes back with rustling shade
And apple-blossoms fill the air —
I have a rendezvous with Death
When Spring brings back blue days and fair.

It may be he shall take my hand
And lead me into his dark land
And close my eyes and quench my breath —
It may be I shall pass him still.
I have a rendezvous with Death
On some scarred slope of battered hill,
When Spring comes round again this year
And the first meadow-flowers appear.

God knows 'twere better to be deep
Pillowed in silk and scented down,
Where love throbs out in blissful sleep,
Pulse nigh to pulse, and breath to breath,
Where hushed awakenings are dear . . .
But I've a rendezvous with Death
At midnight in some flaming town,
When Spring trips north again this year,
And I to my pledged word am true,
I shall not fail that rendezvous.

ALAN SEEGER (1888–1916)

Fleurette

THE wounded Canadian speaks:

My leg? It's off at the knee,
Do I miss it? Well, some. You see
I've had it since I was born;
And lately a devilish corn.
(I rather chuckle with glee
To think how I've fooled that corn.)

But I'll hobble around all right.
It isn't that, it's my face.
Oh, I know I'm a hideous sight,
Hardly a thing in place.
Sort of gargoyle, you'd say.
Nurse won't give me a glass,
But I see the folks as they pass
Shudder and turn away;
Turn away in distress . . .
Mirror enough I guess.
I'm gay! You bet I *am* gay
But I wasn't a while ago.
If you'd seen me even today,
The darndest picture of woe,
With this Caliban mug of mine,
So ravaged and raw and red,
Turned to the wall — in fine
Wishing that I were dead . . .
What has happened since then,
Since I lay with my face to the wall,
The most despairing of men!
Listen! I'll tell you all.

That *poilu* across the way,
With the shrapnel wound in his head,
Has a sister: she came today
To sit awhile by his bed.
All morning I heard him fret:
'Oh, when will she come, Fleurette?'

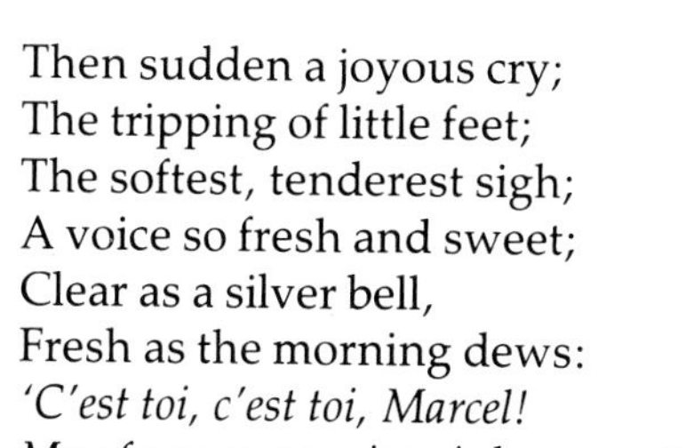

Then sudden a joyous cry;
The tripping of little feet;
The softest, tenderest sigh;
A voice so fresh and sweet;
Clear as a silver bell,
Fresh as the morning dews:
'C'est toi, c'est toi, Marcel!
Mon frere, comme je suis heureuse!'

So over the blanket's rim
I raised my terrible face,
And I saw — how I envied him!
A girl of such delicate grace;
Sixteen, all laughter and love;
As gay as a linnet, and yet
As tenderly sweet as a dove;
Half woman, half child — Fleurette.

Then I turned to the wall again.
(I was awfully blue, you see),
And I thought with a bitter pain:
'Such visions are not for me.'
So there like a log I lay,
All hidden, I thought, from view,
When sudden I heard her say:
'Ah! Who is that *malheureux*?'
Then briefly I heard him tell
(However he came to know)
How I'd smothered a bomb that fell
Into the trench, and so
None of my men were hit,
Though it busted me up a bit.

Well, I didn't quiver an eye,
And he chattered and there she sat;
And I fancied I heard her sigh —
But I wouldn't just swear to that.

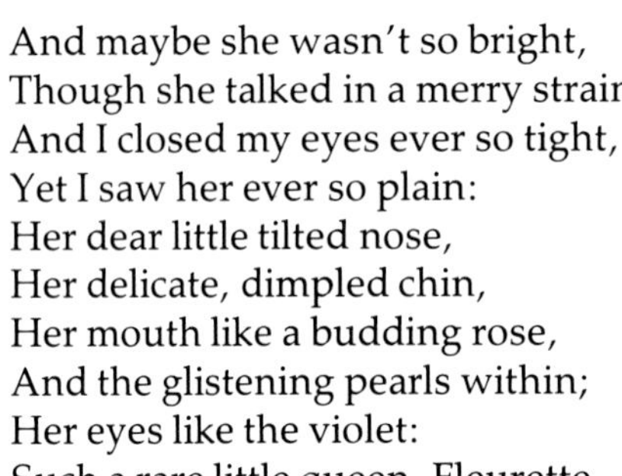

And maybe she wasn't so bright,
Though she talked in a merry strain,
And I closed my eyes ever so tight,
Yet I saw her ever so plain:
Her dear little tilted nose,
Her delicate, dimpled chin,
Her mouth like a budding rose,
And the glistening pearls within;
Her eyes like the violet:
Such a rare little queen, Fleurette.

At last, when she rose to go,
The light was a little dim,
And I ventured to peep, and so
I saw her, graceful and slim,
And she kissed him and kissed him, and oh
How I envied and envied him!

So when she was gone I said
In rather a dreary voice
To him of the oppposite bed:
'Ah, friend, how you must rejoice!
But me, I'm a thing of dread.
For me nevermore the bliss,
The thrill of a woman's kiss.'

Then I stopped, for lo! she was there,
And a great light shone in her eyes.
And me! I could only stare,
I was taken so by surprise,
When gently she bent her head:
'May I kiss you, sergeant?' she said.

Then she kissed my burning lips,
With her mouth like a scented flower,
And I thrilled to the fingertips,
And I hadn't even the power
To say: 'God bless you, dear!'
And I felt such a precious tear
Fall on my withered cheek,
And darn it! I couldn't speak.

And so she went sadly away,
And I know that my eyes were wet.
Ah, not to my dying day
Will I forget, forget!
Can you wonder now I am gay?
God bless her, that little Fleurette!

ROBERT SERVICE (1874–1958)

All the Hills and Vales Along

ALL the hills and vales along,
Earth is bursting into song,
And the singers are the chaps
Who are going to die perhaps.
   O sing, marching men,
   Till the valleys ring again.
   Give your gladness to earth's keeping,
   So be glad, when you are sleeping.

Cast away regret and rue,
Think what you are marching to.
Little live, great pass.
Jesus Christ and Barabbas
Were found the same day.
This died, that went his way.
   So sing with joyful breath,
   For why, you are going to death.
   Teeming earth will surely store
   All the gladness that you pour.

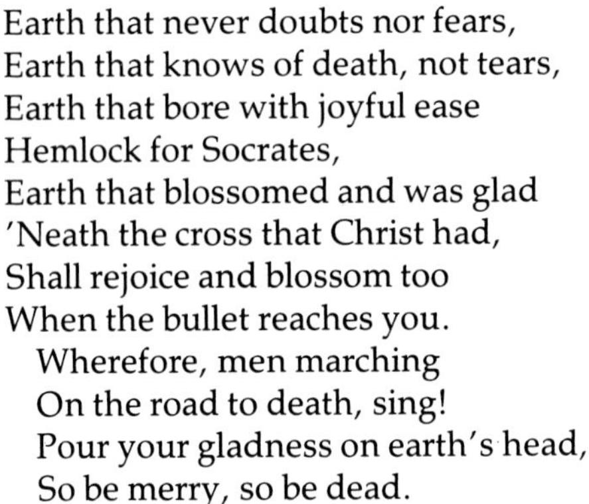

Earth that never doubts nor fears,
Earth that knows of death, not tears,
Earth that bore with joyful ease
Hemlock for Socrates,
Earth that blossomed and was glad
'Neath the cross that Christ had,
Shall rejoice and blossom too
When the bullet reaches you.
   Wherefore, men marching
   On the road to death, sing!
   Pour your gladness on earth's head,
   So be merry, so be dead.

From the hills and valleys earth
Shouts back the sound of mirth,
Tramp of feet and lilt of song
Ringing all the road along.
All the music of their going,
Ringing swinging glad song-throwing,
Earth will echo still, when foot
Lies numb and voice mute.
   On, marching men, on
   To the gates of death with song.
   Sow your gladness for earth's reaping,
   So you may be glad, though sleeping.
   Strew your gladness on earth's bed,
   So be merry, so be dead.

CHARLES HAMILTON SORLEY (1895–1915)

HUMOUR AND SATIRE

The Vicar of Bray

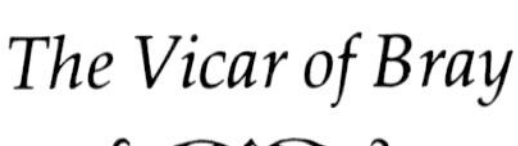

In Good King Charles's golden days,
When loyalty no harm meant,
A furious High Church man I was,
And so I gained preferment.
Unto my flock I daily preached,
'Kings are by God appointed,
And damned are those who dare resist,
Or touch the Lord's Anointed.'
And this is law, I will maintain
Unto my dying day, Sir,
That whatsoever king shall reign,
I will be Vicar of Bray, Sir!

When royal James possessed the crown,
And Popery grew in fashion,
The penal laws I hooted down,
And read the Declaration:
The Church of Rome I found would fit
Full well my constitution,
And I had been a Jesuit,
But for the Revolution.
And this is law, etc.

When William our deliverer came
To heal the nation's grievance,
I turned the cat in pan again,
And swore to him allegiance:
Old principles I did revoke,
Set conscience at a distance,
Passive obedience is a joke,
A jest is non-resistance.
And this is law, etc.

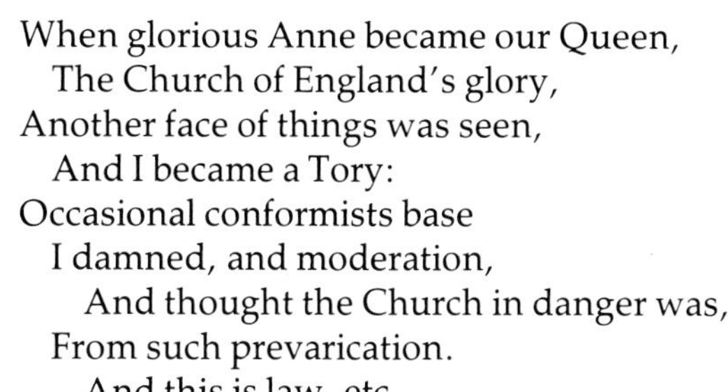

When glorious Anne became our Queen,
  The Church of England's glory,
Another face of things was seen,
  And I became a Tory:
Occasional conformists base
  I damned, and moderation,
    And thought the Church in danger was,
  From such prevarication.
    And this is law, etc.

When George in pudding time came o'er,
  And moderate men looked big, Sir,
My principles I changed once more,
  And so became a Whig, Sir:
And thus preferment I procured
  From our Faith's Great Defender,
    And almost every day abjured
  The Pope and the Pretender.
    And this is law, etc.

The illustrious House of Hanover,
  And Protestant Succession,
To these I lustily will swear,
  While they can keep possession:
For in my faith and loyalty
  I never once will falter,
    But George my lawful King shall be,
  Except the times should alter.
    And this is law, etc.

ANON

To Ironfounders and Others

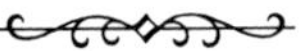

WHEN you destroy a blade of grass
You poison England at her roots:
Remember no man's foot can pass
Where evermore no green life shoots.

You force the birds to wing too high
Where your unnatural vapours creep:
Surely the living rocks shall die
When birds no rightful distance keep.

You have brought down the firmament
And yet no heaven is more near;
You shape huge deeds without event,
And half-made men believe and fear.

Your worship is your furnaces,
Which, like old idols, lost obscenes,
Have molten bowels; your vision is
Machines for making more machines.

O, you are buried in the night,
Preparing destinies of rust;
Iron misused must turn to blight
And dwindle to a tetter'd crust.

The grass, forerunner of life, has gone,
But plants that spring in ruins and shards
Attend until your dream is done:
I have seen hemlock in your yards.

The generations of the worm
Know not your loads piled on their soil;
Their knotted ganglions shall wax firm
Till your strong flagstones heave and toil.

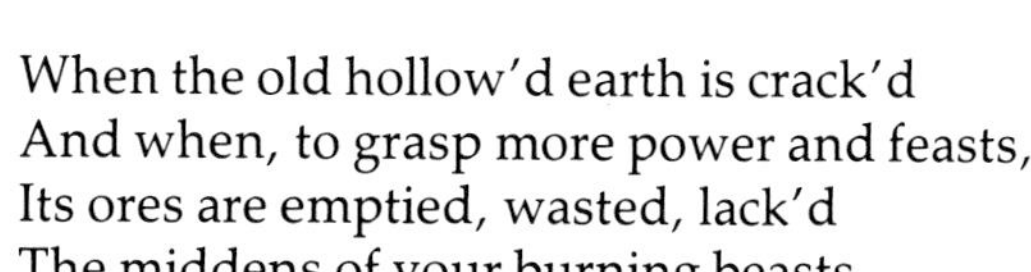

When the old hollow'd earth is crack'd
And when, to grasp more power and feasts,
Its ores are emptied, wasted, lack'd
The middens of your burning beasts

Shall be raked over till they yield
Last priceless slags for fashionings high,
Ploughs to wake grass in every field,
Chisels men's hands to magnify.

GORDON BOTTOMLEY (1874–1948)

The Soldier's Reply to the Poet

('Will it be so again?')

SO THE Soldier replied to the Poet,
Oh yes! it will all be the same,
But a bloody sight worse, and you know it
Since you have a hand in the game:
And you'll be the first in the racket
To sell us a similar dope,
Wrapped up in a rosier packet,
But noosed with as cunning a rope.
You coin us the catchwords and phrases
For which to be slaughtered; and then,
While thousands are blasted to blazes,
Sit picking your nose with your pen.
We know what you're bursting to tell us,
By heart. It is all very fine.
We must swallow the Bait that you sell us,
And pay for your Hook and your Line.
But his pride for a soldier suffices
Since someone must carry the can;
In war, or depression, or crisis,
It's what you expect of a man.
But when we have come to the Isthmus
That bridges the Slump to the War,
We shall contact a new Father Christmas
Like the one we contacted before,
Deploring the one he replaces
Like you do (it's part of the show!)
But with those same mincing grimaces
And that mealy old kisser we know!
And he'll patent a cheap cornucopia
For all that our purse can afford,
And rent us a flat in Utopia
With dreams for our lodging and board.

Salvador Dali (1904–1988) *Man with Head Full of Clouds,* Edward James Foundation, Sussex

Marc Chagall (1887–1985) *The Acrobat,* Private Collection

And we'll hand in our Ammo and Guns
As we handed them in once before,
And he'll lock them up safe; till our sons
Are conscripted for Freedom once more.
We can die for our faith by the million
And laugh at our bruises and scars,
But hush! for the Poet-Civilian
Is weeping, between the cigars.
Mellifluous, sweeter than Cadbury's,
The M.O.I. Nightingale (Hush!)
Is lining his pockets with Bradburies
So his feelings come out with a rush,
For our woes are the cash in his kitty
When his voice he so kindly devotes
In sentiment, pathos and pity,
To bringing huge lumps to the throats
Of our widows, and sweethearts, and trollops,
Since it sells like hot cakes to the town
As he doles out the Goitre in dollops
And the public is gulping it down.
Oh well may he weep for the soldier
Who weeps at a guinea a tear,
For although his invention gets mouldier,
It keeps him his job in the rear.
When my Mrs the organ is wheeling
And my adenoids wheeze to the sky,
He will publish the hunger I'm feeling
And rake in his cheque with a sigh:
And when with a trayful of matches
And laces, you hawk in the street,
O comrades in tatters and patches,
Rejoice! since we're in for a treat:
For when we have died in the gutter
To safeguard his income and state,
Be sure that the Poet will utter
Some beautiful thoughts on our Fate!

Roy Campbell (1901–1957)

RIJP

I Saw a jolly hunter
With a jolly gun
Walking in the country
In the jolly sun.

In the jolly meadow
Sat a jolly hare.
Saw the jolly hunter,
Took jolly care.

Hunter jolly eager —
Sight of jolly prey —
Forgot gun pointing
Wrong jolly way.

Jolly hunter, jolly-head —
Over-heels gone.
Jolly old safety-catch
Not jolly on.

Bang went the jolly gun.
Hunter jolly dead.
Jolly hare got clean away.
Jolly good I said.

Charles Causley (1917–)

Poets

It Isn't a very big cake,
some of us won't get a slice,
and that, make no mistake,
can make us not very nice
to one and all — or another
poetical sister or brother.

We all want total praise
for every word we write,
not for a singular phrase;
we're ready to turn and bite
the thick malicious reviewers,
our hated and feared pursuers.

We feel a sad neglect
when people don't buy our books;
it isn't what we expect
and gives rise to dirty looks
at a public whose addiction
is mainly romantic fiction.

We think there's something wrong
with poets that readers *read*,
disdaining our soulful song
for some pretentious screed
or poems pure and simple
as beauty's deluding dimple.

We can't imagine how
portentous nonsense by A
is loved like a sacred cow,
while dons are carried away
by B's more rustic stanzas
and C's banal bonanzas.

We have our minority view
and a sort of trust in Time;
meanwhile in this human zoo
we wander free, or rhyme,
our admirers not very many —
lucky, perhaps, to have any.

GAVIN EWART (1916–)

A Slice of Wedding Cake

Why have such scores of lovely, gifted girls
  Married impossible men?
Simple self-sacrifice may be ruled out,
  And missionary endeavour, nine times out of ten.

Repeat 'impossible men': not merely rustic,
  Foul-tempered or depraved
(Dramatic foils chosen to show the world
  How well women behave, and always have behaved).

Impossible men: idle, illiterate,
  Self-pitying, dirty, sly
For whose appearance even in City parks
  Excuses must be made to casual passers-by.

Has God's supply of tolerable husbands
  Fallen, in fact, so slow?
Or do I always over-value woman
  At the expense of man?
                                        Do I?
                                                        It might be so.

Robert Graves (1895–1985)

Toads Revisited

Walking around in the park
Should feel better than work:
The lake, the sunshine,
The grass to lie on,

Blurred playground noises
Beyond black-stockinged nurses —
Not a bad place to be.
Yet it doesn't suit me,

Being one of the men
You meet of an afternoon:
Palsied old step-takers,
Hare-eyed clerks with the jitters,

Waxed-fleshed out-patients
Still vague from accidents,
And characters in long coats
Deep in the litter-baskets —

All dodging the toad work
By being stupid or weak.
Think of them!
Hearing the hours chime,

Watching the bread delivered,
The sun by clouds covered,
The children going home;
Think of being them,

Turning over their failures
By some bed of lobelias,
Nowhere to go but indoors,
No friends but empty chairs —

No, give me my in-tray,
My loaf-haired secretary,
My shall-I-keep-the-call-in-Sir:
What else can I answer,

When the lights come on at four
At the end of another year?
Give me your arm, old toad;
Help me down Cemetery Road.

PHILIP LARKIN (1922–1985)

Bagpipe Music

IT'S NO go the merrygoround, it's no go the rickshaw,
All we want is a limousine and a ticket for the peepshow.
Their knickers are made of crêpe-de-chine, their shoes are
made of python.
Their halls are lined with tiger rugs and their walls with
heads of bison.

John MacDonald found a corpse, put it under the sofa,
Waited till it came to life and hit it with a poker,
Sold its eyes for souvenirs, sold its blood for whiskey,
Kept its bones for dumb-bells to use when he was fifty.

It's no go the Yogi-Man, it's no go Blavatsky,
All we want is a bank balance and a bit of skirt in a taxi.

Annie MacDougall went to milk, caught her foot in the
heather,
Woke to hear a dance record playing of Old Vienna.
It's no go your maidenheads, it's no go your culture,
All we want is a Dunlop tyre and the devil mend the
puncture.

The Laird o' Phelps spent Hogmanay declaring he was
sober,
Counted his feet to prove the fact and found he had one
foot over.
Mrs Carmichael had her fifth, looked at the job with
repulsion,
Said to the midwife 'Take it away; I'm through with
over-production'.

It's no go the gossip column, it's no go the Ceilidh,
All we want is a mother's help and a sugar-stick for the
baby.

Willie Murray cut his thumb, couldn't count the damage,
Took the hide of an Ayrshire cow and used it for a
bandage.
His brother caught three hundred cran when the seas
were lavish,
Threw the bleeders back in the sea and went upon the
parish.

It's no go the Herring Board, it's no go the Bible,
All we want is a packet of fags when our hands are idle.

It's no go the picture palace, it's no go the stadium,
It's no go the country cot with a pot of pink geraniums,
It's no go the Government grants, it's no go the elections,
Sit on your arse for fifty years and hang your hat on a
pension.

It's no go my honey love, it's no go my poppet;
Work your hands from day to day, the winds will blow
the profit.
The glass is falling hour by hour, the glass will fall for
ever,
But if you break the bloody glass you won't hold up the
weather.

LOUIS MACNEICE (1907–1963)

My Enemies Have Sweet Voices

I WAS in a bar called Paradise
the fiddler from the band
                    asked me, 'Why do you stand
here crying?'
                    I answered him: 'Musician,
this may come as a surprise —
I was trying to split the difference
when it split before my eyes.'

My enemies have sweet voices
their tones are soft and kind
when I hear my heart rejoices
and I do not seem to mind.

I was playing brag in Bedlam
the doctor wouldn't deal
                    asking, 'Why does he kneel
down weeping?'
                    I answered him, 'Physician,
I think you would have cried —
I was falling back on failure
when the failure stepped aside.'

My enemies have sweet voices
their tones are soft and kind
when I hear my heart rejoices
and I do not seem to mind.

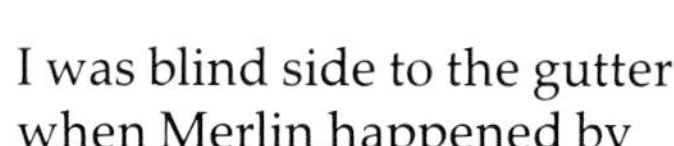

I was blind side to the gutter
when Merlin happened by
asking, 'Why do you lie
there bleeding?'
I answered him, 'Magician,
as a matter of a fact
I was jumping to conclusions
when one of them jumped back.'

My enemies have sweet voices
their tones are soft and kind
when I hear my heart rejoices
and I do not seem to mind.

Pete Morgan (1939 –)

Jolly Good Ale and Old

I Cannot eat but little meat,
My stomach is not good;
But sure I think that I can drink
With him that wears a hood.
Though I go bare, take ye no care,
I nothing am a-cold;
I stuff my skin so full within
Of jolly good ale and old.
Back and side go bare, go bare;
Both foot and hand go cold;
But, belly, God send thee good ale enough,
Whether it be new or old.

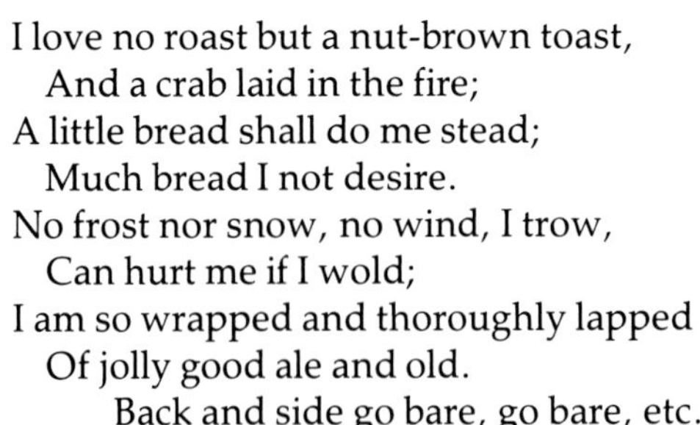

I love no roast but a nut-brown toast,
   And a crab laid in the fire;
A little bread shall do me stead;
   Much bread I not desire.
No frost nor snow, no wind, I trow,
   Can hurt me if I wold;
I am so wrapped and thoroughly lapped
   Of jolly good ale and old.
      Back and side go bare, go bare, etc.

And Tib, my wife, that as her life
   Loveth well good ale to seek,
Full oft drinks she till ye may see
   The tears run down her cheek:
Then doth she trowl to me the bowl
   Even as a maltworm should,
And saith, 'Sweetheart, I took my part
   Of this jolly good ale and old.'
      Back and side go bare, go bare, etc.

Now let them drink till they nod and wink,
   Even as good fellows should do;
They shall not miss to have the bliss
   Good ale doth bring men to;
And all poor souls that have scoured bowls
   Or have them lustily trolled,
God save the lives of them and their wives,
   Whether they be young or old.
      Back and side go bare, go bare;
      Both foot and hand go cold;
      But, belly, God send thee good ale enough,
         Whether it be new or old.

JOHN STILL (1543–1608)

The Sorrows of Werther

WERTHER had a love for Charlotte
  Such as words could never utter;
Would you know how first he met her?
  She was cutting bread and butter.

Charlotte was a married lady,
  And a moral man was Werther,
And for all the wealth of Indies,
  Would do nothing for to hurt her.

So he sigh'd and pined and ogled,
  And his passion boil'd and bubbled,
Till he blew his silly brains out,
  And no more by it was troubled.

Charlotte, having seen his body
  Borne before her on a shutter,
Like a well-conducted person,
  Went on cutting bread and butter.

WILLIAM THACKERAY (1811–1863)

INDEX OF POETS

INDEX OF FIRST LINES

ACKNOWLEDGEMENTS

Permission to use copyright material is gratefully acknowledged to the following:

Faber and Faber Ltd for *Night Mail* by W H Auden; John Murray (Publishers) Ltd for *A Subaltern's Love-Song* by John Betjeman from *Collected Poems;* Peters Fraser and Dunlop Group Ltd for *Almswomen* by Edmund Blunden; Stainer & Bell Ltd, London, England for *Lord of the Dance* by Sydney Carter; David Higham Associates Limited and the author for R I J P by Charles Causley; Jonathan Cape Ltd for *Leisure* by W H Davies; Faber and Faber Ltd for *The Journey of the Magi* by T S Eliot from *Collected Poems 1909–1962;* Victor Gollancz Ltd for *Poets* by Gavin Ewart; Jonathan Cape Ltd for *Pan With Us* by Robert Frost; A. P. Watt Limited on behalf of The Executors of the Estate of Robert Graves for *A Slice of Wedding Cake* by Robert Graves from *Collected Poems 1975;* David Higham Associates for *One Flesh* by Elizabeth Jennings from *Selected Poems* published by Carcanet; Faber and Faber Ltd for *Toads Revisited* by Philip Larkin from *The Whitsun Weddings;* Andre Deutsch Ltd for *April Rise* by Laurie Lee; Allen & Unwin Ltd for *Goodbye* by Alun Lewis; Faber and Faber Ltd for *Bagpipe Music* by Louis MacNeice from the *Collected Poems of Louis MacNeice;* The Literary Trustees of Walter de la Mare and The Society of Authors as their representative for *The Listeners* by Walter de la Mare; The Society of Authors as the literary representative of the Estate of John Masefield for *Sea-Fever* by John Masefield; David Higham Associates Limited for *For Johnny* by John Pudney from *Collected Poems* published by Shepheard Walwyn; Faber and Faber Ltd for *Aftermath* by Siegfried Sassoon; The Society of Authors on behalf of the copyright owner, Mrs Iris Wise for *In the Poppy Field* by James Stephens; David Higham Associates for *And Death Shall Have No Dominion* by Dylan Thomas from *The Poems* published by Dent; and The Bridgeman Art Library for the paintings opposite pages 16, 17, 32, 33, 48, 49, 65, 80, 81, 96, 112, 113; Demart Pro Arte BV/Dacs 1989 for the painting opposite page 128 and ADAGP, Paris and Dacs, London 1989 for the painting page 129.

Whilst every effort has been made to trace all copyright holders the publishers apologise to any holders not acknowledged.